Praise for NO BETTER MEDICINE:

The Critter Lady has done it again, writing a book that only the Critter Lady could write! NO BETTER MEDICINE is chock-full of entertaining stories about cats, ducks, horses, mice, and other colorful critters. Kelly has great insight into animals!
-Bob Tarte,
Author of
* Enslaved by Ducks
* Fowl Weather
* Kitty Cornered

In NO BETTER MEDICINE, Kelly Meister-Yetter shows the reader how cats, dogs, and other assorted critters are an integral part of her healing journey. Her candid and engaging writing, and heartwarming stories, offer hope for others on a similar path.
-Ingrid King
Publisher and founder of The Conscious Cat
Award-winning author of
* Buckley's Story: *Lessons from a Feline Master Teacher*

NO BETTER MEDICINE

*How caring for critters helped
heal the wounds of the past*

KELLY MEISTER-YETTER

In Loving Memory Of
Johnny Moffett -
a man who never got old.

ACKNOWLEDGEMENTS

Much gratitude goes to Whoville's Animal Control Officer Dave, for all his help, over the years, along with his boundless cheer. A grateful shout-out to Whoville Director of Important Things Jon Watson, for being part of the solution. Many thanks to the kind folks at South Suburban Animal Hospital, Brannan Veterinary Hospital, and Bird & Exotic Wellness Center, for taking such great care of all my critters. A special thank-you to fellow critter writers Bob Tarte and Ariel Wulff, for sharing their time and wisdom. Belated thanks to Dorri Jacobs for her superlative editing job. Love, thanks, and endless appreciation to my wonderful and ever-so-patient husband Duddy, who builds a mean duck pen!

And, as always, thank you Jean Cook. Without whom.

The most haunted of houses is the human mind.

- Patrick McGrath

TABLE OF CONTENTS

PREFACE

As any writer will tell you, coming up with a good book title is just as important as what the book's about. You can write a great book, but with a dud of a title, who will want to read it? But while choosing a title for my first book (*Crazy Critter Lady*) was fairly easy, the title for the sequel eluded me.

I came up with a couple of ideas and bounced them off my friend, *Enslaved by Ducks* author Bob Tarte. I can always count on Bob to cut right to the heart of any matter we're discussing, so when he nixed my ideas, I did, too. When I settled on *No Better Medicine*, though, I didn't ask for any opinions. My gut felt it was the right title, and I trust my gut. But the subtitle – *How Caring for Critters Helped Heal the Wounds of the Past* – was a different matter.

As a childhood sexual abuse survivor, I pay close attention to every news story that involves children being molested. The Jerry Sandusky case alone caused me a number of sleepless nights because he had the arrogance to try to blame the very victims he'd abused. Unlike that disgusting creep Sandusky, I know firsthand how those children suffered, and I know firsthand how they continue to suffer as adults.

And therein lies the rub: that while caring for critters has, indeed, helped my recovery enormously, *there is no cure for having been molested.* There is no cure for the inevitable depression that ensues. There is no cure for the Post Traumatic Stress Disorder that tears our lives apart. And I don't want anyone coming to a different conclusion simply because the subtitle sounds upbeat. The fact of the matter is, I continue to be haunted on a daily basis by what happened over forty years ago.

In spite of over twenty years-worth of therapy (including alternative therapies, hypnosis, and dozens of medications), I still suffer from frequent nightmares whose recurring theme is that a man is trying to kill me. Until recently, when I acquired the roommate who is now my husband, I forced myself out of bed after every one of those nightmares, intent on surveying the entire house, making sure that no one was actually in it. There was no way I could go back to sleep until I had checked every single room.

I continue to suffer from trust issues, impulse control issues, retail therapy (read: shopping) issues, and anger issues. The word "issue" is an easy one to bandy about, and an easy one for the reader to gloss over, but the fact is that all of those issues are debilitating to one degree or another. And, it goes without saying that I continue to suffer from issues in the bedroom. What most people take for granted, sex-wise, remains an uphill battle for me well into my fifties.

But for those of you who have also suffered at the hands of a sick, twisted pervert, the news isn't entirely bad. There *is* a measure of healing to be had. It takes work, it takes time, and it takes a good therapist to help you, but it *is* possible to rise above the mire of self-loathing, alcoholism, drug addiction, and other problems that arise because of the past. For you, healing may be found in religion, or the arts, or a career. For me, it was helping animals. And as my healing continues, so does my commitment to critters.

I would be entirely remiss if I didn't mention the wonderful man who looked beyond the difficulties that plague me and saw someone worth building a life with. Because of his enduring love and patience, I'm able to work through some of my more tenacious issues and wrestle them into submission. There's no doubt in my mind that I will always suffer flashbacks, nightmares, and depression, but with Duddy beside me, I'm no longer alone in my struggle; I have the love of my life cheering me on. Well, I have the love of my life, four cats, eight ducks, and a barn full of ornery horses cheering me on. How cool is that?!

Kelly Meister-Yetter
Whoville, Ohio 2014

A Little Wind

To say that the evening in question was "a dark and stormy night" would be to flirt dangerously with understatement – not to mention cliché. But the fact of the matter is that the night of June 5 was, indeed, a dark and stormy one. My Facebook friend Norm, who seems to take a perverse delight in being the bearer of bad news, gleefully updated the dire warnings issued by the Weather Channel online as the massive storm cell raced across the Midwest, leaving a huge trail of destruction in its wake.

My immediate concerns were the things I had no control over: the gang of abandoned ducks I looked after, living shelter-less, and helpless, at McKinnon's Pond; the rescue horses at the barn where I volunteer, whose stables lay directly in the path of the storm; and, of course, my own five cats – three of whom had chosen to hide God only knew where when the wind started to blow.

The storm had already spawned numerous tornadoes before it even hit the Ohio line, and it was headed directly toward the Critter Shack. The warning sirens sounded as I stood at the sliding glass door, peering out into the darkness. The gusting winds alone were terrifying: my home huddles beneath a huge maple tree, and one of my worst fears has always been that a storm would blow the thing right onto the house.

I had managed to sequester Spanky and Junebug in the bathroom. I had no idea where Buddy, Muffin and Gracie were, and I fervently hoped that they had chosen safe places to ride out the storm. As the minutes ticked by, my worry over the errant felines grew, but there was simply no time to conduct a thorough search for them.

Due to the small window above the tub, the bathroom wasn't a particularly safe room to hide from a tornado in, but it seemed the likeliest option. I alternated between pacing the small space and going out into the family room for periodic updates from the t.v. It was as I paced around the toilet that I heard the roar of thunder. Except that it wasn't thunder at all: thunder claps are fairly brief; what I heard continued to roar for several minutes. It was then I realized that what I was actually hearing was a tornado.

I dropped to the floor and huddled next to the toilet. I remember saying numerous prayers to the Gods to please send that thing elsewhere, that now was not a good time for me to die. Time seemed to hang, suspended. There was no way to tell where the tornado was going, although after a couple of minutes of mind-numbing panic, it became clear that the thing had, thankfully, wrought its destruction somewhere other than where I was. In the end, that tornado flattened Lake High School, and a number of houses on Main Street in Millbury, Ohio.

The June 5 tornado made the national news for a variety of reasons, not least of which was the fact that the Lake High School seniors had been set to graduate – in the high school – the very next day. In addition, one student's father was killed by the storm. This was devastating news to Millbury and the surrounding communities: in this neck of the woods, we're all small town folk, and one family's loss is every family's loss. We were all horrified by the level of destruction, and help came immediately for everyone afflicted by it.

I, myself, felt incredibly lucky: not only were all five cats safe – the errant three came out of hiding an hour or so after the storm passed – but when I went outside to inspect the damage the next day, I was amazed to find that not one shingle, not one leaf, was out of place. It was as if the storm had never passed my way. My gratitude to the Gods was immeasurable, so it seemed like the right thing to do to go and view the damage that others had suffered. Sometimes, bearing witness is all that you *can* do.

A few days after the storm, I drove over to Millbury. Slowly, I picked my way up Main Street, swerving around the debris as best I could, while my head swiveled this way and that. The destruction was incomprehensible: one ranch house had been untouched by the storm but for the decorative brick wall out front that had been knocked over. Right next door, the house was gone completely, leaving behind little evidence that it had ever existed; only the foundation remained.

In the woods behind the houses, the trees had been stripped bare. It was a shocking sight, the branches completely devoid of leaves. They looked somehow prehistoric. It was a sight I would see time and again as I followed the path of destruction over two counties.

The most disturbing sight of all, though, was the L-shaped house, still intact, with a girl's pink bike jammed into the corner where the two halves of the house met. The wind had picked up the bike and flung it to the second floor where it hung, suspended, in that corner. That image still haunts me.

My first phone call, the day after the storm, was to The Harmony Barn, where I volunteer. The barn rescues abused and neglected horses, and all throughout the storm, my mind had conjured images of beloved cranky donkey Cricket swirling through the air like that house in *The Wizard of Oz*. Co-owner Ron assured me that the horses and buildings were safe, that the tornado had veered off-course at the last minute, away from the property. Having been a member of the township fire department, Ron had already made the rounds of the surrounding country roads, taking stock of who needed what, and helping out where he could.

It was Ron who told me about the house that had been lifted off its foundation, turned a few feet, and set back down. None of the doors would shut properly; all the jambs were out of plumb. I had seen something similar with someone's garage: it had been picked up, turned in a similar fashion, and set back down without any other trace of tornado damage. It seemed that destruction came in all shapes and sizes, none of which made any logical sense.

Two weeks after the June 5 tornado, Bad News Norm posted another weather warning on Facebook: a virtually identical storm cell was tearing across the Midwest, wreaking similar havoc to the same areas that had already been hit fourteen days prior. As the wind picked up again, I felt a strange panic course through my veins: it was the sort of PTSD that one would expect from actual tornado victims, not from someone who had escaped the destruction. But I felt it nonetheless, and realized that there was no way I could endure Round Two huddled next to my toilet. Out of sheer desperation, I ran next door to neighbor Russell's house.

Owing to my propensity for depression-induced isolation, I had lived next to Russell for three years before I found out that he and I had actually graduated from the same class at the same high school. He was a good neighbor in that he lived a quiet life, and he let me swim in his pool any time I wanted. Neighbors don't get much better than that!

Russell's front door was open, and as I peered in through the screen door, I could see him sprawled out on his couch watching t.v. "Russell," I hollered, "Have you seen a weather report?"

"Why? Is there some weather going on out there?"

"Jesus, Russell," I squawked at him, "There's a flippin' tornado coming *right this way!*"

I walked into the house as he surfed through the channels, and paced around his coffee table. "Why are you so nervous?" he asked.

"Russell! Do you not remember the last tornado that came through here? Big thing, took out a few houses?"

"It was just a little wind," he said calmly, "Here, have the rest of my wine cooler!"

"Thanks," I replied, as he handed me the bottle. I took several large swigs before steering the conversation back to the subject at hand. "Where can I hide? You got a basement?" Russell rolled his eyes at that.

"How about I hide in your hallway, then? There aren't any good hiding places at my house." I strode purposefully toward the interior of his home as I said it. It wasn't perfect, but it would do in a pinch. I remained there for some minutes, waiting for whatever might happen.

When the wind picked up, so did Russell's interest in the matter. I peered around the corner of the hallway, watching, horrified, as he walked out the front door. He stood looking around his driveway as if he was daring the twister to come his way. Only a man would do such a dumb thing during a tornado warning! I waited for the storm to teach him a lesson, but of course, that never happens when you want it to! Instead, he sauntered back into the house and stood staring at me. "Well?" I asked anxiously, "Did you see any houses flying by?"

"Relax," he said as he turned back toward the couch, "It's just a little wind!"

Thankfully, storm #2 veered off in other directions as well, sparing myself, my house, my five cats, the pond ducks, the rescue barn full of horses, and that ornery donkey, too.

EVERYONE'S FAVORITE DONKEY

Surviving the June 5 tornado – and its sequel two weeks later – provided everyone in the area with an exercise in gratitude, and nowhere was this more apparent than at The Harmony Barn. Ron and Wendy knew exactly how fortunate they'd been in dodging the twisters, and we volunteers were equally heartened that no harm had come to our 20-some charges. And while we loved every critter in the barn equally, in the immediate aftermath of the storms, almost everyone inquired about one resident in particular: *"Is the donkey o.k.?"*

Of all the equine residents at The Harmony Barn, the least friendly animal turned out to be everyone's favorite: Cricket the donkey. Cricket came to the rescue barn by way of Kenny the Tiger Guy. Kenny was a local fellow who rescued exotic animals. At any given time, he played host to numerous big cats, bears and wolves. Naturally, feeding all those animals was a full-time occupation, and Kenny gratefully accepted just about every donation he got – except for healthy animals.

It's an ugly fact of life that not every horse owner is a loving, caring owner: there are far too many who own horses for no other reason than to be able to brag that they own horses, and there are those who consider their horses nothing more than mere property to do with as they please. Cricket the donkey belonged to someone in that last category.

The story I heard was that the owner had hoped to breed donkeys, and intended for Cricket to be the brood mare. Cricket had other ideas though: due to a substantial facial injury, Cricket didn't want anyone coming up behind her – least of all an unwelcome stud – which put the kibosh on the breeder's plans pretty quickly. Apparently disgusted by the lack of cooperation, he donated Cricket to Kenny.

The owner knew full well what Kenny would do with the donation, but he clearly didn't concern himself with the matter. Kenny, on the other hand, found that he could not, in good conscience, slaughter an animal whose only fault was being unwanted. So he called The Harmony Barn. Wendy agreed to take Cricket, and all the volunteers looked forward to meeting her. We had no idea what we were in for.

No one knows how Cricket's face came to be injured. Wendy, who prefers to put a positive spin on things, said she hoped that the injury was accidental, rather than intentional. Whatever happened, the bones under Cricket's left eye had been broken and never healed properly. They jutted out enough to impair her vision somewhat, rendering her wary and easily startled. It's entirely likely that the injury caused her chronic pain, as well; it would certainly account for the dark moods she experienced, although we wouldn't come to know about those for some time.

It was common for a new resident – particularly one who hadn't been treated well elsewhere – to be reserved for a while after arriving at the barn. They often took that time to get the lay of the land, assess the herd, and try to figure out their place in it. We volunteers always embraced new arrivals enthusiastically, showering them with treats and attention, grooming them and braiding their manes. The shyer rescues endured the attention meekly, too afraid to do anything but stand there and take it. Others simply walked away when they'd had enough. When Cricket finally got her bearings, she did neither; she plowed right through us instead.

Once the honeymoon period of reserve had ended, it became apparent that Cricket was moody and unpredictable. This struck an endearing chord in the more inexperienced among us because we had no idea just how dangerous a cranky donkey could be. We simply thought that some soothing words and a carrot or two would take care of the problem. As it turned out, they did not. Indeed, they only served to make her more demanding during her moody periods. At those times, if she couldn't get what she wanted from someone, she would literally toss them aside with a flick of her misshapen head. She was surprisingly strong in that regard.

Wendy issued periodic edicts about not hand-feeding the donkey, but almost everyone ignored them, including me. That willful refusal to follow the rules had its own consequences, though, as I discovered the day I walked around the mud lot being chased by Cricket. I wasn't unduly alarmed until she reared up on her hind legs, flailing her front hooves at me and making strange *nuh-nuh-nuh* noises in the bargain. I was at a complete loss for what to do.

In the distance, I heard Wendy shout, "hit her," which sent my fear factor into overdrive: Wendy would *never* tell someone to hit one of her animals unless there was a damn good reason. In this case, the damn good reason turned out to be my personal safety. Evidently, Wendy had been through this sort of thing before with Cricket, and knew it would end badly for me if I didn't do something.

So I whacked the side of Cricket's face with my open hand. It did nothing to stop the onslaught. As Cricket reared up a second, and then a third, time, I turned sideways and dove through the strands of electric fence, rolling to a harmless stop on the other side.

It had been a close call, and it had been my fault. I stood up, and with some embarrassment brushed the dirt off my jeans while assuring Wendy that I was o.k. I hated looking like a complete amateur, and resolved to take Wendy's rules about Cricket more seriously in the future.

While we volunteers generally respected Wendy's decrees, Cricket had her own rules, and woe to the unsuspecting person who unwittingly disobeyed them! When she lost patience, Cricket thought nothing of running right over someone, chasing them down an aisle, or quite possibly biting their leg. Many times, I had seen Cricket pin her ears and tilt her head downward toward someone's ankle. While that behavior always shocked me, Wendy remained unfazed, and with shrug and a toss of her head would say, "That's what happens when you hand-feed them."

Contrary to what you might think, Cricket *did* have some endearing qualities. There were times when she enjoyed interacting with us, standing still, as she would, while one of us spent many minutes scratching her back. She liked being groomed, and on many occasions, sought us out for companionship by joining us in the stalls when we cleaned them. More often than not, she'd stand unmovable in the doorway, blocking our attempts to leave the stall.

While Wendy and the younger volunteers seemed to find Cricket's desire to keep them company in the stalls a bit vexing, and you could frequently hear one of them saying, "*Move, Cricket!*," I personally enjoyed her presence.

Like me, Cricket was emotionally damaged, and, like me, Cricket experienced moods in which she preferred to be alone, which made any interest in friendship on her part all the more poignant.

There was one thing that Cricket did *not* like, and that was baths. We didn't know that, though, the day Wendy – casting about for ways to occupy the younger volunteers – suggested we give one to Cricket. Indeed, Wendy sounded like she knew from experience that this would be something that Cricket would love. Her optimism turned out to be woefully misplaced.

I stood holding onto the lead rope as one of the children hosed Cricket down. When they lathered her up, Cricket began to move about, side-stepping and circling around me in an effort to get away from them. The longer they tried to bathe her, the more agitated she became until she finally, simply, broke free and took off running up the driveway.

I was still holding onto the lead rope at the time. Racing along behind her, trying desperately hard not to lose my grip on the rope, I began hollering over my shoulder for Wendy. She finally appeared from inside the barn and stood staring at us with a look of bemusement on her face. "Don't let go!" she called out, and it was clear that she was trying hard not to laugh. Half-way up the driveway, Cricket's run slowed to a walk, and I managed to steer her back toward the barn. I was *not* amused.

In subsequent years, that episode with Cricket became my talking point every time Wendy tried to suggest something similar. If she claimed that a certain horse might like to be groomed, my retort was always, "Sure, and Cricket likes getting a bath!" When she insisted that one of the famously-ornery horses had an easy-going nature, I replied, "Right, just like Cricket and those baths she loves!" I never missed an opportunity to point out how I'd risked my life chasing down a pissed-off donkey, and Wendy never missed an opportunity to have a good laugh about it. Somewhere in the middle lay our mutual affection for what we all suspected was the world's worst donkey.

THE GANG

In addition to my volunteer duties at the barn, there was the self-appointed task of looking after the McKinnon's Pond ducks. These were the flightless domestic ducks who had been dumped there after they'd stopped being cute Easter ducklings. Over the years, I had come to arrangements with both Whoville's Director of Important Things – who kept the pond fountain running every winter for the simple reason that he liked the ducks, and Whoville's Animal Control Officer Dave – who helped me keep the population under control by searching out domestic duck nests every spring so that I could change out the eggs for useless chicken eggs from the store. As it turned out, though, I had other helpers I initially never knew about.

It was Officer Dave who gave me the phone number of the woman who had called him to report an injured duck. Pat Mitchell certainly got the details right when she mentioned the large Black Swede with the limp, and Dave knew that I would have more answers than he did: while Dave was a huge help during nesting season, he left the rest of the ducks' care to me. Indeed, by the time I called Pat, the duck in question had already received veterinary care, and enjoyed a brief stay in my bathroom. He was still convalescing there when I spoke to her.

"He's going to need a new home," I told Pat, "he won't survive the winter on that slippery pond ice with his limp." Unfortunately, I didn't know anyone that wanted a duck, and I was drawing a complete blank as to what to do next when Pat shocked me by offering to house Ducky in her garage until spring. Reassuring me that she and husband Pete could meet all his needs, she invited me to bring Ducky over. We set a date for two days hence, and I spent the time fretting about whether I'd done the right thing. I'd never met these people, after all – indeed, never even knew they existed until our phone call. As it turned out, I needn't have worried.

Upon arrival at the Mitchell's house, the first thing I saw was the inside of the garage. They'd already created a cozy straw nest for Ducky inside a large critter cage. A few feet away was a child's plastic wading pool, filled with water. Brick steps had been set up inside the pool and out, for easy entrance and exit. Additional straw had been strewn about the garage floor as well. It was the perfect set-up.

When I released Ducky from the carrier, he made his way into the straw-filled cage. Pat crouched down on her hands and knees, adjusting his food and water bowls as she talked, explaining to Ducky that this was his new winter home. He seemed to digest the information, and as I watched the two of them, it dawned on me that Ducky probably wouldn't be going back to the pond come spring. I was clearly witnessing the start of a new friendship, and that suited me just fine: one less domestic duck living with the daily threat of extinction at the jaws of area predators was one less domestic duck I had to worry about. I breathed a sigh of relief as I headed home.

During my visit with the Mitchells, Pat had mentioned that she and Pete regularly fed the McKinnon's Pond ducks. Over time, she'd gotten to know the domestics well enough to tell them apart. As she spoke, I worried that the ducks would get too much food from too many sources, and I hinted to Pat that they might benefit from a diet, but I don't think Pat ever practiced any portion control. It was just as well come winter anyway, when the ducks' usual sources of supplemental foods – worms, bugs, and fish – dried up or froze over. On days when the weather was ghastly, and the road from Middlebridge, where I lived, to Whoville, where the ducks lived, became impassable, I came to rely on the Mitchell's close proximity to the pond and stayed home, relieved that the ducks would still get a decent meal in my absence.

In addition to the Mitchells, I learned that I had another duck-feeding volunteer named Liz. She sent me an email one day, announcing that her boyfriend lived near McKinnon's Pond, and that she would be happy to feed the ducks if I so desired. I immediately jumped on the offer and thanked her profusely: now I had a weekend feeder, and could save myself the gas my car consumed driving between the two towns. Things were coming together nicely!

When I was two years old, my paternal grandmother walked in on my father while he was molesting me. There were angry words, hissed quietly so that no one else in the house would hear. It was decided that I was too young to remember what happened. I was not. My grandmother believed she could control the situation. She could not. The one thing she could have done to save me – report my father, tell someone, <u>anyone</u> – she did not do. Consequently, my father continued to molest me for ten more years.

MISS MUFFIN

The old woman had named her Heidi. I don't know how long they were together, but by the time the woman had surrendered the cat and gone into a nursing home, Heidi was three years old. I don't know how long Heidi had been at the shelter, either, but her behavior the day I met her suggested that she was more than ready to begin a new life with someone else.

At the time, I wasn't looking for another cat. I had just lost Kitty, my special feline friend of fourteen years, and was grieving deeply when my therapist suggested that I visit the local humane society. Evidently, she thought that being around all those critters would cheer me up.

I wasn't looking for another cat as I perused the kitten cages. They were adorable, of course, but in the depths of my current depressed state, I had no energy for adopting a kitten. I had been petting one of them, anyway, and was just putting the little puff ball back in his cage, when I happened to notice the couple standing on the other side of the room. They had been visiting with a large grey tabby, and were in the process of trying to coax it back into its cage. The tabby wasn't co-operating, though; instead, she casually turned away from the cage and started walking around the room.

I wasn't looking for another cat when I said to the couple, "If you're finished, I'll visit with her for a while." As they left the room, I picked up the tabby, sat down on a chair and plopped her on my lap. She immediately curled up and began to purr. It was then that she said the thing I always wait to hear before deciding to adopt: she said, in a Vulcan mindmeld sort of way, *take me home, Kelly, I'll go home with you!* I wasn't looking for another cat, but she found me anyway.

In my estimation, she wasn't really a Heidi. She was more of a Muffin, which is what I named her. Once I'd brought her home, it soon became clear that the old woman had established some rules that Heidi had obediently followed: never once did she jump on my couch, bed, or any other piece of furniture. And when I offered her a plateful of tuna fish, she refused to eat it. Mystified, I scraped the tuna into her food bowl instead, and watched as she devoured every last bit. As I watched her eat, I concluded that some new rules were in order – namely, non-rules. Mi casa su casa; my couch is your couch.

While Muffin eventually embraced the idea of napping on softer surfaces than the floor, she remained every inch a lady. Indeed, one of my many nicknames for her was *Lady Cat*. She never tried to sneak out the door, she never clawed up the furniture, and she never complained. She became a quiet fixture in whatever home we lived in: always there, but unobtrusively so.

There were always other cats in residence besides Muffin. At the height of my Crazy Cat Lady phase, there were five altogether: Muff, Buddy, Spanky, Junebug and Gracie. Muffin adjusted to Buddy and Spanky very well, taking both kittens under her wing, as it were, and raising them to adulthood. Junebug and Gracie she rejected out of hand; apparently, she'd had enough of playing Mommy Cat. Because the other four had more boisterous personalities, it often seemed like Muffin got overlooked. I always knew she was there, though. She was the only cat who would snuggle up on the couch with me for a nap.

The years passed, as they always do, with little to mark the milestones besides Dick Clark's *Rockin' New Year's Eve*. I moved several times, but I never moved anywhere that the cats couldn't go. There were minor periodic feline illnesses – respiratory infections, UTI's. There were Christmas stockings filled with catnip mice and the cans of wet food that I never fed them otherwise. In Muffin's case, there were occasional strolls around the grounds of the chicken coop we lived in, and the Critter Shack we subsequently moved to. I enjoyed those excursions, and Muffin did, too.

She would stay so reliably close to me during our walks that she was the only cat in the house that didn't require a leash and harness. I would carry her outside, set her down in the grass, and then walk a few feet away. She would wait until I paused to race toward me, stopping just short of crashing into my legs. She would look around, then, raising her face to catch the scents being carried in on the breeze. Muff was a gentle cat, whose quiet nature lent a peaceful aspect to my otherwise chaotic life.

When we moved to the Critter Shack, something odd happened. For reasons I'll never know, she took an immediate dislike to the bedroom. Previously, she had joined the other cats in sleeping on the bed with me, but in the new house, she was having none of it. Every now and then, I'd pick her up and put her on the bed, hoping as I did so that *this time*, maybe she'd feel differently. She never did. She would growl inexplicably, then jump off the bed and leave the room. In the last three years of her life, she never once slept with me again. While you'd think that four other cats would be enough to get me through the night, I missed Muffin's dignified presence on the bed.

It was as I watched t.v. one April evening that I happened to notice Muff's labored breathing. She was napping on the ottoman, and when I glanced down at her, I saw how her sides heaved up and down as she breathed. I didn't really know what to think, and it didn't seem to be something that required immediate attention, so I went back to the t.v. and forgot about it.

When several weeks went by and I realized that Muff's breathing was still labored, I made an appointment with Dr. Henny at Suburban Care Animal Center. I was fairly certain, in that blissfully ignorant way that pet owners tend to be, that there wasn't anything wrong with her that the doctor couldn't fix. You would think that by now, having owned – and lost – several critters, that I would know better than to be so woefully optimistic, but I did not.

The day before we went – a sunny spring day full of the promise of even better weather to come – I took Muffin outside for a walk. We hadn't been out since the previous fall, and ordinarily Muff would relish the opportunity to bask in the sun and claw a few trees. Instead, though, as I followed her with my camera, shooting an impromptu video, she seemed very delicate: carefully placing one paw in front of the other, she lowered herself gingerly to the ground and simply lay there, as though moving required too much effort. I remember saying, for the benefit of the camera that was still recording, *"I don't know if she'll be around much longer."* As it turned out, I was much closer to the mark than I realized.

Dr. Henny looked her over carefully as I explained the reason for our visit. I agreed to her suggestion that we do an x-ray, and I sat with Muffin on my lap as we waited for the results. The doctor was very gentle in her explanation that Muff had fluid built up around her heart and lungs, making it hard to breathe. She said that she could drain the fluid, but that it would simply build up again. In her opinion, the kindest thing to do was euthanize.

I'd been down this road before. Even worse, I'd seen – back in the days when Dr. Green was my vet and my friend Sam the vet tech had made me privy to details about other people's pets – how, all too often, folks couldn't face putting their pet down, and would often take the animal home again instead, regardless of the fact that it might be suffering. Long ago, I had vowed to always put the critter's needs first, and not my own. If the doctor said it was time to euthanize, then that's what I did, and I dealt with my feelings about it later. Sadly, it was time to make that decision once again.

The staff quietly withdrew from the exam room, giving me time to say my good-byes. As anyone who's had to euthanize a pet already knows, there's never enough time to say that good-bye. The staff could leave you in the room all afternoon and it still wouldn't be long enough. How long I held Muffin, I have no idea. I stroked her fur, kissed her head, and repeatedly told her what a special Lady Cat she'd been all those years. When the staff came back in to do the procedure, I told them I wasn't ready yet.

I told them the same thing afterward, too. Dr. Henny had put the stethoscope on Muff's chest, declared that her heart and breathing had stopped, extended her sympathies and then left the room. A vet tech came in some time later to take the body, and it was then that I said it again. *"I'm not ready!*" I wailed through my tears, and heard the door shut quietly behind me. I knew I'd have to hand Muffin over at some point, though, so I spent the last few minutes with her inhaling her scent, trying desperately hard to memorize every feature of her being, and knowing that it was already too late; that she was gone and it was time to let the tech take her away for cremation. Feeling desolate, I quickly left the building and sobbed all the way home.

Ever since that day, I've had a measure of guilt gnawing at me – gnawing because she never once wanted to sleep in the bedroom of the Critter Shack with me; gnawing because of all the times that the noisier cats, like that proverbial squeaky wheel, got the lion's share of attention while quiet Muff stayed in the background, waiting her turn; gnawing because of how fast those eleven years had gone by, and how much of the daily feline minutiae I'd missed for one reason or another. Gnawing because I feel certain that I somehow *could've done better by her.*

There are a number of pictures of Muffin in the house. Being a photographer, I'm accustomed to recording the lives of the critters around me. Everywhere I look – on the bookshelf in my office, on the console next to the t.v., on the wall of the family room – are reminders of the life I shared with Muff. And while I'm glad to have those reminders, looking at them is so painful that I rarely do it. It's the same with my memories of her: the loss is so excruciating that I can't bear to think about her. Out of emotional necessity, the door to that mental room remains closed.

If I've learned nothing else about the all-too-short lives of the critters in our care, I've learned this: that every day is to be cherished in some way. Even if it's nothing more than stopping to take note of the fact that your pet licked your hand, or smiled at you, or jumped up on my chair to keep me company while I cried my way through writing this chapter, *those are the moments you'll need to sustain you later, when you, too, have to say that awful good-bye.* Don't wait until it's too late, make time out of your busy life now, today, this minute, to cherish your special critter. And, be sure to take plenty of pictures! You'll never regret giving your beloved pets extra attention. Indeed, your only regret will be in not giving them enough.

TOLERATING THE
OCCASIONAL HUMAN

Over the years, an untold number of volunteers passed
through the doors of The Harmony Barn. Some came spo-
radically. Some came only once and, when they discovered
that there wasn't going to be nearly as much riding as there
was poop scooping, never returned. Some came and left an
indelible mark on the place. Mandy Schmidt was one of the
latter.

I confess that I wasn't initially very hospitable toward
the other volunteers. I was there to learn about horses, after
all, not deal with irritating humans. Kids were the worst:
oftentimes, parents would drop them off in what was obviously a bid for some free babysitting. That trick usually only
worked a few times, though, before the child in question decided that mucking out stalls on a Saturday morning was not
their idea of fun. One girl was so obnoxious that she would
repeatedly clap her hands at the horses, demanding that

they approach her. She refused to believe me when I told her that her behavior was actually scaring them off.

Over time, I became aware of the fact that several kids of varying ages kept coming back week after week, month after month. They did a decent job cleaning the stalls, and I never once heard any of them complain about the work. This core group – Allen, Lydia, Olivia and Mandy – earned my grudging respect because they rarely missed a Saturday. No matter how hot in summer, or how cold in winter, they almost always turned up, ready to do what needed to be done.

The oldest was Mandy. A senior in high school, Mandy brought plenty of previous horse experience with her to the barn. She'd done 4-H, taken riding lessons, *and* cleaned stalls at another barn in exchange for leasing one of the horses. She was a nice kid from a nice family, always kind to the younger children and always polite with barn owner Wendy.

We had a few conversations about nothing in particular, and she struck me as an intelligent young woman. She did well in school and planned on studying speech pathology in college. She didn't seem to date much, or distract herself with the sort of things that got other kids into trouble. All in all, she was a likeable girl. That nice persona harbored a mischievous side, though, as I soon found out.

I had a birthday coming up, and Wendy asked me how old I'd be. As was the custom, we were all standing around chitchatting before settling into the day's work. "Forty-seven," I replied. The volunteers all drifted off to their assigned duties without comment.

Some time later that morning, Mandy – who must've been thinking about this for a while before she dared to say it – inquired, "So, what's it like being that old?" I glanced over in time to see the evil grin that had spread across her face.

"What's it like being you?" I retorted.

"I kinda like it!" she replied.

"I don't doubt it!"

I exacted my revenge a few weeks later, when one of the older volunteers announced that her daughter had won a $40,000 scholarship to college. Turning immediately to Mandy, I remarked, "Too bad you're not that smart!" Her grin returned, only this time, instead of evil, it was clearly a grin of appreciation that she'd finally found someone who was willing to give as good as she got. Our opening salvos turned out to be the beginning of a very agreeable friendship.

She had a thing about mental illness. I found this out during one of our stall-mucking conversations. For reasons I never understood, there was something about crazy that unsettled her. I only learned this because one of her high school homework assignments had her reading my all-time favorite book, *One Flew Over The Cuckoo's Nest*. "It's a great book!" I exclaimed, "you're gonna love it!"

"I already don't like it," she announced.

"It's a *classic!* Trust me!" Boy, was she pissed off when she read the part where Chief Broom kills McMurphy!

"You said I'd like it!" she argued angrily a few weeks later.

"Can I help it if craziness freaks you out?" The funny part was, a year later, when she was in college, one of her professors made the class sit through the movie!

"I can't believe I have to do this *again!*" she moaned, "it *sucks!*"

Sighing heavily, I explained, "You're totally missing the point of the thing. It's not *about* mental illness, it's about conformity versus non-conformity. When that book was written, there was a huge gulf between the conformists in this country – who believed that we were all supposed to think and live a certain way, and the non-conformists – who wanted to explore other possibilities. Did you know," I lectured, veering off on a tangent, "that when people converged on Washington to protest the Vietnam War, President Nixon ordered that buses be parked all around the White House so he wouldn't have to see the non-conformists outside?"

Mandy looked at me dubiously, clearly wondering whether I'd made my point yet. "McMurphy represents the non-conformists of the world, and Nurse Ratched represents the conformists. So, in the end, who's right – the guy who wants to live outside the pre-formed box, or the nurse who believes that everyone should spend their entire lives inside that pre-formed box? That's all I'm sayin'."

"It still sucks," she stated flatly.

"This is why I work with critters: because humans are an aggravating lot. Not unlike yourself."

The evil grin returned: "Did you ever march in those protests?" she asked in her best attempt at looking innocent.

"Why you....*I'm not that fucking old!*" She collapsed into helpless laughter, then.

"This is what I like about you," she said when she'd recovered, "you always have a comeback. You're the only person I know that I can mess with like this!" Indeed, that was exactly what I liked about her, too.

PRETTY BOY DUCK

The McKinnon's Pond ducks enjoyed a relatively lengthy spell of good health before the next disaster presented itself. Squatting down in my usual duck-feeding posture one fall day, I noticed some horrific, unidentifiable problem with Pretty Boy's left eye. It looked to me like his whole eye was just gone altogether, so I seized the opportunity and grabbed the duck. Domestic ducks can put up quite a fight when they want to, but I somehow managed to stuff him into the critter carrier I always have in the trunk of my car. Because the ducks tended to schedule their emergencies for the days when our primary vet is off work, I had to drive him forty minutes across town to the Exotic Critter Clinic.

Dr. Susan hmmm'd and uh-oh'd while she looked Pretty Boy over. His eye was still there, thank God, but his lower lid had been badly torn. Dr. Susan said she wanted to keep him overnight to work on reducing the swelling, and then try to stitch him up the next day. Knowing that Pretty Boy was in good hands with this avian specialist, I didn't worry too much about the outcome. I agreed with Dr. Susan's assessment, and I liked the sound of her plan.

When I picked him up late the next day, his eye looked 100% better: the swelling had gone down, and the stitches had put everything back together nicely. Dr. Susan ordered ten days of eye drops twice a day, and said he was ready to go back to the pond. She actually preferred that he spend the winter in a nice cozy barn, but since I didn't have one of those, I was pretty emphatic about him going home to the pond where he belonged.

I had every confidence in my ability to grab him up at least once a day and get the drops in him – mostly because I forgot about the mob mentality among the ducks. If one of them has an issue, then suddenly everyone does. And on Day Three of Operation Eye Drops, the whole gang decided that they'd had enough of this grabbing business.

They didn't like the idea of one of their fellows being manhandled, dragged off against his will, and undoubtedly beaten and tortured for days or weeks – even if he was really only gone the couple of minutes it took me to put him in the carrier and administer the drops. No, those jumbo-sized Pekins were convinced that there was evil afoot and its name was "*Kelly.*"

So they stopped coming near me at the feeds. Each and every one of those stinkers stayed at least eight feet away from me. To add insult to injury, they quacked at me the whole time, too. "Go away now, Kelly!" they said firmly, over and over again in a deafening duck chorus, "Won't let you touch us!" Jeez! Now what?!

I was pretty p.o.'d at myself for being so over-zealous as to try to give Pretty Boy the eye drops twice a day. Even Dr. Susan had said, "Twice a day is best, but once a day is better than nothing." I should've known better than to disrupt the normal once-a-day feeding routine. I should've just attempted the drops once a day and left it at that. I should've, but I didn't. Fortunately, the ducks had short memories and didn't hold grudges against evil Kellys, so on Day Six, I was able to get near them again. Pretty Boy's eye looked great, and I was thrilled to be back in the ducks' good graces. That thrill would be very short-lived.

On Day Seven, Pretty Boy's stitches — along with the flap of skin they were supposed to be holding in place — were flapping in the breeze. Oh God! What happened? With the benefit of hindsight, I think it was nothing more complicated than Pretty Boy scratched his itchy eye, and the sharp little hooks on the underside of his foot accidentally yanked the stitches out. However it happened, it happened — yet again — on Dr. Chrys's day off and we had to drive all the way across town again to see Dr. Susan.

It wasn't as bad as it looked, and in fact, Dr. Susan was able to trim off the flap of skin underneath Pretty Boy's eye and re-stitch the remainder. She was pretty firm about him getting all his drops this time around, though, and suggested I put him up in my garage. Great idea, but I didn't have one! Dr. Susan's staff had done some homework in my absence, though, and knew a woman who'd be willing to keep Pretty Boy in her barn for the winter.

I balked at the idea. I didn't know who the barn woman was, or whether I'd ever see my favorite duck again if I handed him over to her. And besides, apart from the eye injury, Pretty Boy had a good thing going at McKinnon's Pond. He had siblings there, and numerous friends. Heck, he even had a girlfriend! They had a pond the size of a small lake to swim in, and Jon Watson, one of the Big Cheeses who worked for the City of Whoville, was such a fan that he was willing to keep the fountain going in the pond all winter long, just so those ducks had open water to swim in. How could a barn possibly compare with that?

Even so, there was no getting around the serious fact that Pretty Boy stood to lose his eye if those stitches didn't do their job. And to do their job, he needed drops in his eye twice a day, every day, for at least a week. And if he lost his eye, he'd never be going back to the pond again because he'd be far too vulnerable. At Dr. Susan's prodding, I put my mental gears to work and they only came up with one solution: take him home and put him in my bathroom for a week. Which is just what I did.

Things went well enough for a couple of days. I developed a routine in which I would thoroughly clean the duck-poop-filled bathroom first thing each morning while Pretty Boy spent the time trying to escape from the critter carrier. Once I'd had a shower, I'd fill the tub with water and give Pretty Boy some tub time, several times throughout the day. By Day Four, though, I noticed that he wasn't eating much food and I grew concerned.

I contacted my friend Bob Tarte, a fellow critter writer and duck tender, explaining about Pretty Boy's waning appetite and asking for suggestions on how to remedy it. I detected a note of real concern in Bob's response to my email. He'd probably had some dire outcome with a duck who had eaten poorly, but was afraid to tell me. It was just as well — I didn't want to know the worst-case scenario anyway. But his concern made me a lot more worried than I'd been before: I once had a cat who stopped eating when he was ready to die, and I didn't want Pretty Boy doing the same thing. So off to the store I went to implement Bob's suggestions.

By the time I was finished with Operation Eat Your Dinner, Pretty Boy had a veritable smorgasbord of munchies to choose from: arrayed before him were a pile of grass from the yard, a bowl of cracked corn, a dish of cat kibble, another of fresh fruit chunks, and a bowl of duck pellets. All on my best china, no less, because I'd run out of crappy critter bowls.

He seemed to appreciate the variety: every time I went in to check on him, a little more was missing from the bowls. He sampled the duck pellets with little apparent enthusiasm, while the cat food seemed to be his consistent favorite. The cracked corn usually got eaten, though he appeared to ignore the fruit and the grass altogether. God only knows how Bob convinced his ducks to eat their greens, because it was clear that Pretty Boy had no intention of eating his.

While his appetite became less of a problem, the eye injury became more so. He'd apparently been scratching an itch again because by Day Five, some of the stitches had popped out of place. It was just as well: that flap of skin clearly wasn't getting any blood circulating to it, and I was fairly certain that Dr. Susan would pronounce the attempt at sewing his eyelid back together a failure. His third eyelid seemed to be working harder to protect the eye, but I felt sure that that wouldn't be good enough for the exacting Dr. Susan.

One thing I noticed about Dr. Susan was that conditions and situations had to be perfect. Not merely acceptable, or anywhere outside the box, but *perfect*. Where she would be thinking, "Now you need to find him a nice barn to live in," his usual vet, Dr. Chrys, would be thinking, "He's got that third eyelid to help him out, he should be fine." Two different, well-qualified views on the same subject by two different doctors. To be honest, I much preferred Dr. Chrys's optimism, and privately wished that she was treating Pretty Boy now.

I knew he'd be fine back at McKinnon's Pond, and anyway, I was down there five days a week, keeping a close watch on all the ducks. On my days off, my volunteers would alert me if something was wrong. If a problem cropped up again, I'd be able to help. I knew that Dr. Susan wasn't going to like it, though, the idea of this less-than-perfect critter being sent back to the wild. What had she said early on in his treatment? *Two eyes, two wings, two legs.* Well, Pretty Boy was five for six with that cancerous wing missing, but he had enough parts to get by with, and he clearly missed his fellows. I had told him repeatedly that I would take him back to the pond as soon as possible, and I took that promise seriously.

There were a couple of firsts on the Monday that Pretty Boy was due to be released. For a start, it was the first time I'd ever spent a birthday in the dentist's chair getting a root canal. I'd been dealing with an ever-increasing amount of tooth pain for over a week. It had gotten to the point where I couldn't even eat my expensive after-dinner chocolates. This was pure torture: the box of Lily O'Brien's Sticky Toffees sat there on my kitchen counter innocently enough, but I knew from experience that eating so much as one of them would produce the sort of pain that only a shotgun to the head would relieve. By the time I got to the dentist on Monday, I – a life-long needle phobic – was actually looking forward to a shot or two of Novocaine.

There was a time limit involved with Monday's root canal: I had to get Pretty Boy to Dr. Susan's in an hour and a half, and I didn't want to miss that appointment. The two dentists at the office conferred for some time before reaching a decision. Since it was my birthday, and since the tooth pain meant that cake was out of the question, my dentist decided to at least start the root canal process in the hopes that I'd get enough initial relief to be able to indulge my sweet tooth. It was a kind thing for him to do and, indeed, I was back to stuffing my face with sticky toffees in a matter of hours!

The dentist finished just under the deadline, leaving me with a temporary filling and another appointment to look forward to, and just enough time to get Pretty Boy to Dr. Susan's. Considering the driving distance involved, I gave serious thought to passing on the check-up and just dropping him back at the pond. But after seven days of duck poop all over my bathroom, and duck bites every time I administered his eye drops, I decided that all our efforts needed official closure.

In truth, I was afraid Dr. Susan would want him to spend a few more days at my house. I wasn't particularly confident about that eyelid healing well, and I didn't think she would be, either. But I had promised Pretty Boy that on Monday, he was going home, and I meant to keep that promise. At the same time, though, he and I had been through too much together to ruin his chances now by not following through. So we made the trip across town to Dr. Susan's, which brings us to the other first that I mentioned.

You would think that after seven whole days of togetherness – days in which I had to pick Pretty Boy up every time he went in the tub, and pick him up again to get him out of the tub; days in which I had to put him in the carrier, and hold on to him while I gave him the eye drops; days in which I sat on the toilet lid and talked to him while he splashed around in the water; days in which I conscientiously changed the bathroom lighting from "day" to "evening at a softly-lit pond" via a nightlight; days in which I struggled to find tempting morsels for him to eat – you'd think that after all that, he would be at least somewhat disposed to a small show of affection from me. You'd think that, but you'd be wrong.

The fact is, Pretty Boy never stopped growling at me until he realized I wasn't kidding about taking him back to the pond. I understood: he was in a strange place, he missed Girlfriend Duck and all his pals, the buffet wasn't up to standard, and I was the instrument by which all this unpleasantness had come to pass. I didn't hold the growling against him, but I can tell you this: when Dr. Susan leaned over and kissed Pretty Boy on the head during that final check-up, I was speechless, and more than a little indignant. And it wasn't even so much her kiss — it was the fact that he *let her* do it! The few times I had tried the same thing, I'd gotten nipped in the face for my efforts.

Much to my considerable surprise, Dr. Susan was happy with how Pretty Boy's eyelid had healed, and agreed that he could go back to the pond. She held off removing the stitches, though, saying he should come back for another check in ten days time. When I told her I wasn't sure he'd let me get near him again that soon, she said that was o.k., that eventually, the stitches would dissolve on their own. Either way, it was time to get him back where he belonged.

I drove him straight to McKinnon's Pond, telling him repeatedly along the way that he'd be seeing, "Pretty Lady, and Big Boy, and Ethel, and Peepers, and Ducky, and Girlfriend!" Whether he knew the names or not, he was certainly familiar with the tone of voice I used whenever I spoke those names. He sat thoughtfully in the carrier, tilting his head to look up at me and no doubt hoping like hell that I was a human who kept my word.

I set the carrier on the ground and aimed the open door toward the pond. Pretty Boy did what he always does when I release him – he headed straight for the water. Once in the pond, he did his usual "I'm home!" dance, in which he paddles back and forth, opening and closing his bill but uttering not one sound. It's as if he's too thrilled for words. He passed up that day's feed, but I knew he'd rejoin the crowd in no time.

It was much too quiet at home, then. This was unexpected considering he'd actually made very little noise in the bathroom. Apart from a few hours of splashing in the tub each day, you would never have known a duck was in there. So I didn't understand at first why the place felt so quiet and empty. You'd think I would be glad to have my bathroom back, with no more slimy green poop, and feathers, and cracked corn all over the place. You'd think that, but all I really felt was a disconcerting void.

I'd experienced this once before, when a terminally ill cat that I'd been caring for twenty-four hours a day for over a year finally died. Once he was gone, so was my purpose, my noble endeavor. I had given that wonderful cat everything I had – money-wise, time- and energy-wise, and certainly more love than I knew I was capable of – and between the two of us, we managed to cheat death for quite a while. After he was gone, though, I no longer felt noble, I just felt empty.

And so it was with Pretty Boy, even though he was alive and well with years ahead of him. Once he was back at the pond, I had no place to channel my caring-for-critters energy. I would survive the transition, but first, I spent two very depressed days sleeping until noon.

On the third day, it poured with rain. The ducks don't like any sort of rain-deflecting gear like umbrellas, or even hoods, so there I was, the Crazy-as-usual Critter Lady, hunched down in the rain, cheerfully calling, "Where's Peepers? How ya doin', Lady? There's Freckle!" and enjoying the hell out of things despite the weather. There may be better ways to spend your time, but offhand, I can't think of them.

My father died of colon cancer in his mid-sixties. It was the only decent thing he ever did in his life. Unfortunately, he didn't see fit to make any deathbed confessions, which – sadly – seemed to convince my family that I had made up my molestation claims. The one thing he <u>did</u> do on his deathbed was leave me a large sum of money.

Instead of planning a secure future, I spent several years plowing through the inheritance, uncomfortable with what I saw as just so much more blood money: throughout my life, my father spent significant sums of money on me. It was hush-money, designed to keep me from telling on him. It worked for a while, but I would not remain silent forever.

THE DOG IN
THE FRAME SHOP

While I had any number of critters on my daily or weekly radar, animals also seemed to show up on the periphery of my life on a regular basis. Sometimes it's an injured chipmunk in need of a little TLC, sometimes it's lending Whoville Animal Control Officer Dave an extra set of hands in catching a loose critter, and sometimes – as was the case now – it's a dog-owning acquaintance of mine.

Growing up in a small town gave me a useful grounding in dealing with neighborhood eccentrics and other characters. Whovillians have generally always been pretty tolerant of those who thought or lived outside the box, as long as they didn't infringe on anyone else. The more you get to know those small town characters, though, the more you learn to appreciate the way they add color to your life. Laura the frame shop lady is one of them.

I've known her for years. I first met her when she worked in someone else's frame store. When she opened her own shop, I took my business there. Her boss had never been terribly reliable, and I tend to like it when people keep to a schedule as promised. Now, I don't want you getting the wrong idea about Laura. She's an astute businesswoman, and a fine artist, to boot. She's got great ideas on how to make your art look even better with the right mat and frame, and she's very active at her church, too. In other words, she's an all-around good egg, even if she *did* put a hand-made sign in her shop window that says, "Have A Day." Laura's just cranky enough that it's too far to go to wish that folks have a *nice* day!

Her frame store is located in an L-shaped strip mall. There's a wine shop next door to the left, and a bar next door to the right. Some other shops have come and gone, in the strip mall, but Laura and the booze are still there after all these years! Out in front of her shop, there's a small landscaped island around which the cars circle. The shrubs look a little unloved but I don't think anyone really cares. To be honest, there's an element of urban blight about the place, but it can't be helped: Whoville is smack in the middle of the mid-western rust-belt and a lot of jobs have been lost around here.

Laura's shop has served me well for over fifteen years, now. Early on, she made a decision that put her squarely in the outside-the-box category: she brought her cat to work. It was a long time ago, and I can't recall the cat's name, but I do remember that she was feline leukemia positive. Laura didn't want her infecting the cat at home, so she installed the cat in the frame shop and there it lived for several years. It was a friendly cat, and I gave her lots of attention every time I stopped in. Some time after the cat passed away, Laura acquired one of those football-sized dogs, and every morning, she'd bring the dog to work. Unlike the cat, though, this pet went home with Laura at night.

After the football dog died, Laura found herself in possession of a large rescue dog of indeterminate breeding. She started bringing Maxi to work with her fairly early in their relationship, and Maxi settled into the routine very nicely. Maxi suited Laura's personality: while Laura was a tad curmudgeonly, Maxi was always cheerful; where Laura was laid back and calm, Maxi got excited about the small things, like the UPS delivery guy's arrival. They were the quintessential Frick and Frack.

They spent long hours together in that frame store. Maxi enjoyed lying in front of the plate glass window, watching the world outside, and she always let Laura know when people of interest were in the neighborhood. The moment I'd get out of my car, Maxi would spot me and start barking. She came to know that I would always pet her, and throw some toys around the shop for her. After a few minutes, when Laura and I would get down to business, Maxi would resume her post at the window. A visit from any of the delivery guys was always grounds for enthusiasm because they often brought dog biscuits for her. Seems like everyone around the strip mall knew Maxi!

That landscaped island out in front of Laura's shop came in handy as a toilet for Maxi. Laura would open the door, make sure it was traffic-free out there, and then let Maxi out to do her business. Maxi was sensible enough to know that she was expected to come straight back into the shop when she was finished.

Because of all that time spent together in the shop, Laura and Maxi developed their own language. Laura always knew the difference between Maxi looking at her because someone was coming up the sidewalk, and Maxi looking at her because she needed to go out and pee. For reasons known only to Laura, she taught Maxi to run a lap around her work station before Laura would let her out. All Laura had to do was gesture with her hand, and Maxi would jog once around the station, and then head toward the door. It was hilarious! Laura would be in mid-sentence, get the look from Maxi, wave her hand as she resumed talking, and the next thing you know, the dog is running a lap around the shop!

Because my framing needs are fairly modest, these days, I only get to the shop once or twice a year. I was there recently, and while I waited for Laura to finish a phone call, I knelt down on the floor to give Maxi some belly rubs. I noticed immediately that she'd lost weight, and I said as much when Laura got off the phone. She told me that Maxi had been sick, of late, and they were, in fact, waiting for the lab results from the vet's as we spoke. In a matter of minutes, the vet called, and told Laura that she hadn't found anything terribly alarming in the work-up, but thought Maxi might have an infection in her liver. They would treat her with antibiotics and see how it went. I left the shop assuming that everything would work out, because things always do, don't they? Or at least, they always work out in my head. Reality is another story entirely.

When I returned to the shop a week later to pick up my finished project, I noticed that things were strangely quiet in the parking lot. No barking, no big cheerful dog wagging her tail in the window. Entering the shop, I asked, "Where's the muttley?"

"Retired," Laura answered quietly.

"She's GONE?" I gasped in shock.

"I put her down on Saturday," Laura replied.

The details don't really matter. Suffice to say that it wasn't an infection at all. My guess, from the sound of things, is that Maxi had a tumor that killed her — or would have, had Laura not euthanized her. There was no question but that Maxi was suffering, and Laura absolutely did the right thing. It was just so unexpected, and came on so fast, that

I was momentarily speechless. There's never any time to process these things because they go from bad, to worse, to worst, in the blink of an eye. And now here we were, Laura and I, shaking our heads over how this thing had happened, how quickly Maxi had deteriorated, how fast Laura had had to make such an agonizing decision.

Now, if this had been a big city instead of Whoville, Laura might never have brought any animals to work. If she did, folks probably wouldn't have bothered to get to know them, like I did, like the UPS guy did, like the wine shop guy next door on the left did. And Maxi's passing probably wouldn't have engendered any special notice from the customers. But here in Whoville, when you have a character like Laura who brings her beloved dog to work every day, week in and month out, year after year, you get a little attached to both of them. Which explains why I'm having difficulty maintaining my composure as I write this.

Just last Christmas, Laura – who is a curmudgeonly Christmas Grinch if ever there was one – sent out holiday photos to all of her regular customers. I opened my Christmas card to find a small color picture inside of Laura wearing a Grinch t-shirt, kneeling, with her arm around her best buddy Maxi, who was wearing fake deer antlers. It was the perfect picture of a perfect small town character, one who's loved precisely because she chooses to be a little different from everyone else.

I left the shop subdued, that day. It was hard to leave at all. Laura doesn't open up to just anyone, so I stayed for quite a while, listening, talking, choking up, hugging it out. My heart aches for Laura because I know what she's going through. And because she chose to ignore the conventional rule that says you leave your pets at home when you go to work, I grieve for what is lost: the shop, that humble frame shop in the run-down strip mall in the rust-belt town, will never be the same without Maxi.

If there is a lesson to be learned, here, apart from cherishing every day that you get with your loved ones, I think that it's this: the Gods put people like Laura in our paths to remind us that not everything is meant to be done by the book. Not everyone is meant to think inside the box, or play by the rules. And when we encounter these characters, we should take the time to get to know them – and their dogs – because that's what small towns are all about. Even if you live in a big city!

JUST WHEN YOU THINK YOU KNOW IT ALL!

When I first got involved with horses, in my early forties, I spent several years taking riding lessons on a frustrating old nag named Crazy. She was frustrating because she was forever testing me, challenging my authority, and pretending that she was deaf. Never once did she follow a command without putting up a lot of resistance first, and our conversations tended to go like this:

> Kelly: "Trot, Crazy!"
> Crazy: *Now?*
> Kelly: "Yes, Crazy, trot now!"
> Crazy: *You mean right now?*
> Kelly: "Yes, Crazy, right now!"
> Crazy: *You want me to trot right now?*
> Kelly: "Crazy!!"
> Crazy: *Maybe I could do that for you later.*

It's worth noting that Crazy put me through this misery every single time I rode her. She made me work for every single step she took. In spite of the fact that she was an experienced horse, she delighted in pretending that she had no idea what I wanted, or simply didn't care. I would spend entire circuits around the arena giving her that command to trot, while Crazy did her best to thwart me. And all the while we were engaged in this power struggle, Crazy's circles would get smaller and smaller, until we were basically walking around the middle of the arena, instead of out by the wall where we belonged. It was all very vexing indeed.

After a time, I shelled out for a pair of ball spurs. They helped emphasize my commands, but it took me years to realize that it's not how hard you nudge their ribs, it's how much horsemanship you possess. At that time, I possessed very little; Crazy knew far more than I did. While it's good that someone in the equation knows what they're doing, I would prefer that it be me! And although I spent most of those lessons feeling completely humiliated by my lack of ability, it was in overcoming obstacles that I learned the most.

When Crazy retired from giving lessons, she also retired from being the go-to horse that barn owner Wendy used for the younger volunteers. At that point, Ruckus – a bombproof horse of gentle reliability – was pressed into service. While Ruckus employed his own brand of tactics designed to get him out of doing any actual work, I still managed to get on his back and learn a thing or two during our lessons. Ruckus was nowhere near as aggravating as Crazy had been, and I discovered early on that he had a certain liking for going fast: he was a retired barrel racer who still enjoyed loping a few laps around the arena, and he didn't require the use of ball spurs to get him moving, either!

While Ruckus was now the main go-to horse at the barn, there was another horse in residence that got pressed into service for more experienced people like Mandy. Charlie was a good-looking horse, but his personality left a lot to be desired. As far as I was concerned, he was a sour horse who had no interest whatsoever in making friends with any of us. Why Mandy liked him was a mystery to me.

I spent countless Saturdays watching as she groomed Charlie. Every single time she tried to pick his back hooves, he would flail his legs about in an attempt to kick her. She would always respond in the same fashion, calmly saying, "No kicks, Charlie! No kicks!" while he continued to try to knee-cap her.

"What are you going to do when he finally breaks your leg?" I asked her.

"He won't! He's a good boy!"

"In what parallel universe is Charlie actually considered *good*?"

Mandy would ignore my taunts and, to my considerable surprise, get a decent ride out of Charlie every time she got on him. At the time, I was fairly certain that I would never have a reason to get on his back, but of course, the Gods have a twisted sense of humor, and there came a day when, if I wanted to ride a horse on a given Saturday, I was going to have to get on Charlie.

I don't mind telling you that I felt a fair amount of trepidation when Mandy climbed off (after a ride in which Charlie behaved perfectly), and I took hold of the reins and climbed on. I had no idea what I was in for, but I was pretty sure that it wouldn't be good!

I didn't trust Charlie. After watching all those times he tried to kick Mandy, I had no reason to trust him. I remembered Wendy saying more than once that she never turns her back on him. This from the woman who owns the barn and loves each and every horse that comes through the door! It's not exactly a ringing endorsement. So I climbed gingerly into the saddle, and *tsked* the command for him to walk. He obeyed, walked me once around the arena, and then stopped.

I recalled from lessons I once took on an incredibly stubborn Appaloosa that if the horse refuses to move, you must make a rib-digging irritant of yourself. I tried this tactic with Charlie and it worked. Once. He took a few steps, then stopped again. After that, he was on to me: the trick wasn't going to work twice! I sat there on his back, digging my heels into him, feeling like a complete amateur, and getting nowhere. Wendy and Mandy both called out suggestions – none of which moved Charlie sufficiently to obey – as I sat there wondering why my five-odd years of riding lessons were failing me completely. Just when you think you know what the hell you're doing, someone comes along to remind you that you still have a lot to learn!

Wendy finally came over, took Charlie by the bridle, and led us around like she does with the children. I felt like a complete loser! After some discussion, it was agreed that taking a few lessons on Charlie might not be a bad idea. The thought of spending thirty dollars for the opportunity to be kicked by a nasty horse really didn't appeal to me, but I saw the necessity of it, and made a mental note to steer well clear of Charlie's back legs.

Realizing that those lessons were inevitable, though, got me thinking about how to approach this horse who knows I don't like him. So I hatched a "getting to know you" idea, ran it by Wendy, who approved, and then set the plan in motion. It went like this: every Saturday, after I finished my poop scooping duties, I brought Charlie into the cross-ties and gave him a serious grooming. Wendy told me that he liked being groomed, so it seemed like a good starting point. During those sessions, I even sang a few verses of the theme from the Scooby Doo cartoons, for no other reason than that Temple Grandin, in her fascinating book, *Animals in*

Translation, believes that animals communicate through their own version of music.

When I sought advice from Wendy on how to handle Charlie during grooming sessions, she told me to keep an eye on his ears. Ears are one of the ways horses communicate. If the ears are up and alert, he's listening to you; you have his attention. If his ears are pinned back, he's angry and you want to be very careful: a bite or kick could be coming your way. I lost count of how many times I checked Charlie's ears during those sessions, but I'm pleased to report that he never once flattened them. It was a good start.

There was still a long way to go before I was willing to get on his back again. There was the matter of hoof-picking, which is when he always tried to kick Mandy. While I managed to pick his front hooves without incident, there was no way I was getting near his back legs! I had Wendy do it once, and watched as he flailed his legs at her instead. Sooner or later, I would have to take the plunge and try it for myself, but for now, I decided to stick to grooming his coat. It was time I got to know Charlie, and let him get to know me, and that's a process that can't be rushed.

So, yet again, I was humbled by the fact that a thousand-pound animal reminded me of my limitations. But after Crazy, and the years I spent on Ruckus, maybe that's the problem: that of all the horses in the world, I've only experienced two. Evidently, it's time to expand my horizons. While Charlie wouldn't have been my first choice in that regard, sometimes you're forced to take what the Gods offer you, or miss a valuable learning experience. I chose to take the offer.

LITTLE NIPPER:
THE CASE OF THE
INJURED DUCKLING

Given that the McKinnon's Pond ducks seemed to average about one serious problem a year, I shouldn't have been surprised when, the summer following Pretty Boy's eye problem, one of the ducklings presented me with a challenge unlike any other I'd dealt with before. It involved one of the offspring of Mama Duck, the very same duck who continued to elude the best nest-finding efforts of both myself and Officer Dave. For three years running, she managed to hide her nests so well that we never found them. This year, she hatched eight ducklings. Fortunately for the sake of population control, area hawks and snapping turtles brought the number of remaining offspring down to two. Little Nipper and his sister, Peeps, had managed to survive despite the odds, and were well on their way to adulthood when disaster struck.

I was feeding the gang one morning when I noticed the length of fishing line floating among the ducks. There seemed to be five ducks caught in it, though not so tightly that they couldn't escape. Little Nipper was among those caught, which really tugged at my heart strings: he was just a baby! He was too young for this sort of catastrophe! I held out hope that they would somehow untangle themselves without my interference, and adopted a wait-and-see attitude.

In a matter of days, the ducks managed to disengage themselves, but Nipper now had such a pronounced limp that something was clearly wrong with him, and it was no doubt fishing line-related. His right foot dragged uselessly behind him as he limped along. He was so obviously injured that it was a wonder that a hawk hadn't already made a meal of him. I grabbed him up with a view to taking him to the vet's. He was fairly easy to catch in his compromised condition, and I plopped him gently in the ever-present critter carrier.

Before I drove off, I walked back across the boathouse parking lot, intent on retrieving the bag of cracked corn that I'd left behind during Nipper's capture. It was then that I saw Officer Dave rounding the corner in his Critter Catcher and heading in my direction. He told me he'd gotten a phone call about a duck with some fishing tackle attached to it. I had just finished feeding the entire gang and hadn't seen anything of the sort, which was what I told Dave. I went on to mention the injured duckling, who was at that moment firmly ensconced in the carrier in the front seat of my car. Dave walked over for a look.

He told me then that this was the exact same duckling he'd found tied to a tree a few days earlier. Nipper hadn't really been tied to the tree; he'd accidentally gotten himself wound up in the underbrush because he'd had that fishing line wrapped around his leg. Dave had cut him free, and now, here I was a few days later, taking the poor little guy to the vet. We surmised that the phone call Dave had gotten was probably about Nipper.

There was something about the timing of it all that clearly struck Dave. Here he'd driven to the pond in response to a report of a critter crisis, only to find me already there, a few steps ahead of him! I think it was at that moment that he developed a measure of faith in me that he hadn't had before. We'd always gotten along well in the past, but now, after this particular incident, the realization that I was serious about the animals, and not just some crazy duck broad, seemed to jell in his mind. Before he left, he offered up a fist bump. It spoke volumes.

Dr. Perry, the ducks' new vet, inspected Nipper's leg and told me that the fishing line had caused nerve damage. The line had cut off circulation to his foot for a time, and there was no way to know how much tissue he was going to lose. She was certain that he'd lose some of the webbing in his foot, but also reasonably sure that the foot itself would survive. She gave me antibiotics for the infection and told me that if I hadn't brought him in, the infection would've killed him. Yikes!

It was clear that he was going to need some kind of therapy, not to mention regular doses of the antibiotic, so into my bathroom he went. He was deeply miserable from the start, and remained so for the next seven days. Having been wrenched away from his mother had been a traumatic experience for him – I knew this because as I carried him toward my car, he cried piteously for Mama, who chased along after us for several yards. It broke my heart that I couldn't explain to them that the separation was only temporary.

It became immediately obvious that my bathtub would not be big enough to give Nipper proper hydrotherapy.

I called Pat Mitchell – the volunteer who had adopted Ducky – and asked whether she had anything big enough for a duck to dunk himself in. As luck would have it, she had just the thing: a 52-gallon plastic storage container. It worked perfectly, and once it was filled with water, it became Nipper's hydrotherapy tub.

Hydrotherapy entailed much more than just letting Nipper swim around. It was important that he use his bad leg, so every time I put him in the water, I'd gently pull backwards on a handful of his tail feathers. Because he was afraid of me, he'd pump his little legs extra hard, trying to get away. We'd do that over and over for fifteen-odd minutes at a stretch, then I'd take him in to rest.

Before every round of hydrotherapy, we'd do physical therapy. I should point out here that Dr. Perry never mentioned any of these things during our time in the exam room. We didn't discuss rehab at all. It was something I came up with when it became clear that he wouldn't heal on his own at the pond. So I devised some exercises that I thought would provide the most benefit for a flightless duck.

Physical therapy involved me putting him on a harness and leash – the same ones I'd used to teach my cats to walk with me outside – then letting him walk around the back yard. In truth, he wasn't walking so much as he was running to get away from me. He would race toward the shady areas of my lawn with me following along at his heels. Then I'd pick him up and carry him back to the middle of the yard. When I put him back down on the ground, he was off and running again. Once he'd reach the shade, he'd turn his head, reach around behind him and try to chew the harness off. How he hated every minute of it!

It wasn't just the harness he hated; he hated me, as well. And he told me so, every single day. I'd go into the bathroom in the morning to give him his meds and clean up all the poop and he'd slouch miserably in the corner and announce, "I hate you, Kelly!" It made me sad, but I certainly understood: he was still a baby, missing his mama. And while on some instinctive level, he understood the concept of being eaten by a predator, he had no understanding whatsoever of humans and bathrooms and good intentions.

A new problem developed on Day Three: contracture. Nipper wasn't using the injured foot sufficiently to stave off muscular contracture, so his foot had begun to curl under. I consulted with Dr. Perry, who put the idea in my head when she said there was no point in trying to put a splint on him. To this day, I don't know why she said that, but I'm glad I ignored her.

I discussed the problem with a critter-owning friend of mine and between the two of us, we devised a duck-foot-shaped splint, custom made just for Nipper. We traced his foot around a sheet of plastic, then cut two pieces – one for under his foot, and one for the top. We taped it all together using coach's tape, with his foot sandwiched in between the two pieces of plastic. It worked perfectly! I kept the splint on his foot for a day, making him walk with it on during physical therapy, and the contracture disappeared after less than 48 hours. The splint was a resounding success!

As Nipper continued to improve, and the time to return him to the pond drew near, I began to wonder whether Mama would take him back. Surely, she was used to the idea that once a predator took her young, she was never going to see that duckling again. But what about one reappearing after eight days? I knew that he had imprinted on her, but had she imprinted on him? Did it work both ways, or would she have no idea who he was? The answer mattered to some degree: while he was half-way to adulthood, and could, in theory, get by on his own, he still had a lot to learn about how to be a Big Duck, and Mama was the best duck to learn that from. My questions would have to wait until I took him back to the pond.

The day finally came that I felt comfortable releasing him. Those eight days of rehabilitation had dragged on much more slowly than they normally did with adult ducks. That was probably because I knew the adults were just annoyed by the disruption to their lives, while Nipper was clearly scared and depressed at the separation from his mother. In addition, I think he pooped twice as much as the adults, even while he refused most of the foods the big ducks ate. Because he ate so little while in my bathroom, I ended up worrying as much about him getting a decent meal as I did about successfully rehabbing him. All in all, he ate enough. Not a lot, but enough.

When I released him at the pond, he made a beeline for the water. Swimming in a 52-gallon plastic storage container is not at all the same as swimming in your home water, with all its familiar smells, snacks, and friends. In no time, Nipper found Mama, and while he was overjoyed to see her, her response seemed lukewarm by comparison. I got the distinct impression that she was thinking, "You're *back?* I thought you'd grown up and moved away!" She seemed about as enthused as a human parent would be when their adult child wants to move back home again.

His sister Peeps, who had managed to avoid becoming a hawk snack in his absence, was clearly thrilled to see him, and the two enjoyed a happy reunion. They found one another immediately, and have rarely left each other's sides since. As they grew, they took numerous expeditions around the pond, always finding Mama eventually, but gaining confidence about being Big Ducks in her absence.

Little Nipper walks perfectly well now, without a trace of the limp he still had when I first returned him to the pond. A substantial portion of the webbing on that injured foot became gangrenous. Dr. Perry said that would happen. She advised me to let nature take its course, saying that the gangrenous parts would eventually fall off, which they did. Where the dead tissue had been, there's now a triangle-shaped space that used to be webbing. Nipper swims perfectly well in spite of the missing webbing, and in fact, he's grown to look so much like the duck I assume is his father that that webless area is the only way I can identify him now. Thankfully, he's chosen not to hold a grudge, and bellies up to the bag of corn with all the other ducks.

His was a good rescue, with a great rehab. They don't always turn out this well.

As a childhood sexual abuse survivor, there is much to grieve: I've spent years grieving the loss of What Should Have Been, and the horror of What Actually Was. I've shed more tears than I can count over the course my life has taken, from alcoholism, to disastrous relationship choices, to chaotic friendships and strife within my family. While the animals in my life were a godsend, they have the misfortune to live considerably shorter lives than humans, guaranteeing that I would grieve anew on a fairly regular basis.

THINGS LEFT BEHIND

In the weeks and months after Muffin died, depression took over and dictated how I spent my time. Instead of volunteering at The Harmony Barn as usual, I started sleeping in, rising late in the morning and eating Reese's peanut butter cups for breakfast. Showering was optional, and a proper breakfast didn't get eaten until the afternoon. The clock on the family room wall ticked noisily, serving as a reminder that time drags much too slowly when you're working through grief.

I spent a good deal of time trying to keep myself immersed in busy-work, things designed to keep my hands moving and my brain occupied. The busy-work succeeded at keeping the sadness at bay – for a while. But then the time would come when I had to face reality and deal with the absences: the absence of Muffin's presence, the absence of her meows for attention. The absence of her snuggles with me on the couch. Indeed, there's an entire family room filled with her absences.

No one particularly wanted to be in that room anymore, including me. It's where Muffin spent 99% of her time, the last few years of her life. We all ended up there in the evenings, though – I watching t.v. while the remaining cats kept me company. It felt awkward to be in that room after her death. Many nights, Muffin had joined me on the ottoman, or curled up on my lap in the old Victorian chair, which leaves a big void where she used to be. So now my lap is filled with an absence, too.

Curiously, the dynamic among the cats changed after Muffin's passing. Buddy, the loner, spent less time sleeping and more time checking up on me. Any number of times throughout the day, he would approach me and give me a good sniff. It was nice to see him coming out of his shell more, but it was impossible to explain to him why Muffin was no longer there.

The same was true with Spanky. Immediately after I returned from the vet's, that awful day, I tried to tell Spanky that Muffin had been sickly, so she "had to go." You can read that a couple of different ways, though, and once I realized that, I stopped talking. I didn't want any of the cats thinking that if they got sick, they'd get the boot.

Spanky was the last kitten that Muffin was willing to mother. He was an incredibly needy baby (and, years later, still is), making constant demands of Muffin for attention, for cleanings, for her time. She endured the demands surprisingly well, considering that Spanky was not technically hers – until he grew up. Then she made it very clear that she was done.

Spanky spent the rest of Muffin's life ignoring her growls, and occasionally, his perseverance would be rewarded with a few licks on the head. Spanky would walk away happy, then, clearly believing that his mommy-cat still loved him. Spanky now spends a lot of time asking for my attention. It's a cheap substitute for Muffin, but it'll have to do.

By the time Junebug came along, Muffin had had enough of kittens, and was so nasty to Junebug that I often had to intervene. Muffin had started out life as an only cat, so I understood her unhappiness at being forced to live with so many others, but I drew the line at bullying. Eventually, a certain parity was reached in which I played mommy-cat to Junebug while Muffin found a nice place to nap at the other end of the house. In the aftermath of Muffin's death, Junebug spent a lot of time looking at me as though she wondered if I was o.k. I think she knew that I wasn't.

When Gracie came into the house, everyone tried in their own way to scare her into submission. Gracie was having none of it, though. She'd survived out on the streets with a permanently gimpy leg; she wasn't about to be bossed around by my lot. So they all retreated to the other end of the house to stew about the latest turn of events, and Gracie used the time to find the best place to sleep. Then she spent an inordinate amount of time doing just that.

Muffin and Gracie never cared for each other, which was probably why Gracie spent so much of her time sleeping wherever Muffin wasn't. That all changed after Muff died, though. All of a sudden Gracie chose to spend her evenings in the family room with me and the other cats. It was nice that they all rallied around me and kept me company, but to be honest, I wanted to be anywhere but in that room. There were simply too many reminders of what I lost.

Some time ago at a yard sale, I came across a stuffed, three-dimensional Kliban cat. He's a black and white tabby who's wearing red sneakers. I positioned him on the floor in front of an ottoman that I don't use. For some reason, Muff liked snuggling up to that cat. Now, every time my eyes swept around the family room, they came to rest on that lonely Kliban cat. Another absence.

At a different yard sale, I found a gaudy yellow blanket. It was soft and snuggly, and I rather liked the color. I kept it folded on the family room couch, ready for nap duty. Muffin liked to crawl between the folds, creating a little cat cave for herself. I could always tell by the messy lump where Muffin was sleeping. Now, the blanket lay flat and smooth. Another absence.

In my bathroom there's a set of wicker shelves. I keep two folded beach towels on the bottom shelf. Every so often, Muffin would go in there, paw the top towel until it had unfolded somewhat, and then she'd lie on it. Given that I set up special cat-friendly nooks and crannies all over the house, I have no idea why Muffin liked that spot behind the bathroom door, but she surely did. Now, though, the beach towels are as the gaudy yellow blanket: flat and smooth. Yet another absence.

At some point, there comes a time in the grieving process where you make a conscious decision to move on with life. You scatter the ashes. You go back to work. You put away your loved one's possessions. You start over in a hundred different ways. Your brain begins to adjust to Life After. It doesn't happen at the same time for everyone, but eventually, it does happen.

I'm not there, yet. I'm not even close. My mind doesn't want to make the leap into this new reality of Life After Muffin. I keep looking around the family room, hoping against hope that I'll find her sunning in her usual spot by the sliding glass door. She's not there, of course. She never will be again. And that's the hardest adjustment of all: making your brain understand what your heart doesn't want to accept. Life goes on, as it must, but with one notable difference now: there's a vast emptiness where Muffin used to be. It's a void that can never be filled.

SAYING GOOD-BYE

If grieving the loss of your own beloved pets is hard, grieving for animals that belong to someone else can be tricky. Your own sadness must take a back seat to that of the owners, and no boss is going to give you time off because your friend's dog/cat/whatever died. Fortunately, The Harmony Barn knows how attached we volunteers get to the residents, and every attempt is made to give closure to those who need it. As it happened, I would need that very thing when I least expected it.

I was in the middle of dinner in a restaurant when the phone rang. Noting the name on the Caller ID, I answered my riding instructor's call with, "Who died?" It was the only reason she would call me after hours. I froze, stunned, when I heard her reply, "Cricket."

"What on earth happened?"

"We don't know. She was sick for a few days. Mom thinks it might have been an infection. We'll do a necropsy and see if we can figure it out." She went on to say that there was time for me to come out to the barn and say good-bye before they buried Cricket, which is exactly what I did.

A certain numbness overcame me as I tried to enjoy the rest of my meal, but as I drove through the darkness toward the barn, I allowed the fact of Cricket's passing to fully register, and the tears began to flow. I had just seen Cricket four days earlier. I knew that day that something was wrong because she refused all my offers of snacks, but Wendy assured me that she would be fine.

I had allowed myself to believe her, even though my gut told me otherwise: in less than six months' time, two horses had already died at the barn. Blondie, a boarder horse, had colicked, and then a few months later – and even worse for me personally – my old lesson horse Ruckus had to be put down. His necropsy was inconclusive, but the corn dust the barn had been using for bedding was the suspected cause: since it was ground up corn, the horses ate a fair amount of it. If they didn't drink enough water to wash it through their systems, it could – and most likely did – become impacted.

I was still reeling from Ruckus's death when I got the call about Cricket. I had spent several years taking lessons on him, and even after I moved on to more challenging horses, Ruckus was still one of my favorites: an amiable fellow with a fondness for running fast, I could always count on him to lope me around the arena when he'd finished with the young volunteers. I learned how to post on him. I learned a lot from him: I learned about patience, and trust, with him.

I learned not to be so bossy, to give Ruckus time to respond in his own fashion, rather than getting worked up that he didn't do as I asked right away. I learned when to be firm, and when to cut him some slack. I learned to let Ruckus be Ruckus: once, when I used him in a video I made to promote my book *Crazy Critter Lady,* he pooped on camera. Instead of getting mad, I laughed, and used the footage rather than do the whole video over. Horses poop; what are you gonna do?!

We had a moment, several months before his death, that told me that we had created quite a bond between us. The bond may, in fact, have been there all along, lying dormant until the right situation brought it to the fore. It's entirely possible that I hadn't been paying attention to the state of our relationship. It's a mistake we all make with the critters in our lives: we spend their lifetimes taking for granted that those animals will be with us forever. Or, at the least, for an indeterminate number of years yet to come. And it never occurs to us that today might be the day that that beloved animal dies.

In any case, Ruckus and I had been loping around the arena. After all the kids had ridden him – pulling the reins too tightly, making the mistakes that inexperienced children make – I would climb on and let him run it out. Ruckus liked running, and he seemed to enjoy the opportunity to have at it. We'd lope a few circles in one direction, then turn around and lope the other way. We were right in the middle of this, and sharing the arena with a pony named Piney and his mistress, when one of them accidentally touched the electric fence. The zap it gives you isn't particularly painful, but strangely, you always remember it!

Immediately after the shock, Piney panicked in that way that horses do, tossing the 20-something girl off his back before racing around and around the arena. The minute I saw what happened, I pulled Ruckus to a halt. The safest thing for us to do was stand still and let Piney run it out of his system, which is exactly what he spent the next seven minutes doing. At one point, Piney ran into the corner behind Ruckus and I, standing there as though he was hiding from the girl who stood quietly, waiting for her horse to settle down.

Sometimes, that sense of panic can have a domino effect: the other horses see the one freaking out and figure they'd better do the same. It was to Ruckus's credit that instead of joining Piney in his meltdown, he looked to me for direction instead. An interesting conversation took place then, between Ruckus and I. Not one word escaped my mouth, but we talked nonetheless:

Ruckus: *So, is there a plan, here?*
Kelly: "Yep. We're just gonna stand here for a while."
Ruckus: *That's it? We're just standing?*
Kelly: "That's the plan. We'll just stand here quietly for a while."
Ruckus: *O.k.*

It was the first time that Ruckus not only looked to me for direction in a tight situation, but trusted that I knew what I was doing in the bargain. He finally had enough faith in me to let me take the lead. Ruckus was never a horse to stand still for long, but I'm proud to say that he remained completely still for the duration of Piney's meltdown, pointing one ear forward to keep up with the action, while pointing the other back at me, waiting to hear my next command.

I was so proud of us that day! Proud that I'd learned enough to know that in some situations, your best action is inaction, and proud as hell of Ruckus, who had willingly let me take the lead because he trusted that I could.

That wasn't the only time I was proud of him. In spite of his retired status, a young girl came out to the barn that summer, looking to lease him for the county fair. I watched her a few times as she worked with him. She didn't look like she knew much about horsemanship, but you know what? She took fourth place with him! Boy, was I surprised!

I never let him forget it. Every time the kids and I would groom him, I'd remind him that he was a "Fourth Place Champion Horse!" From somewhere near his hind quarters, I'd hear the kids snickering and I'd admonish them, "There will be no mockage! No mocking the Fourth Place Champion Horse!" Never sure whether I was kidding or not, the kids would quickly swallow their giggles.

He was, of course, more than just a Fourth Place Champion Horse. He was my pal. My buddy. "The best Ruckus in the whole barn!" The kids would laugh at that one, too. They'd roll their eyes and say, "He's the *only* Ruckus in the barn!" "That doesn't make him any less special!" I'd retort.

I'd give him endless snacks. He had a way of thrusting his head out from the cross-ties, eyes wide as saucers. He'd have the most comical expression on his face, as though he'd been starving all this time and just needed *one more* snack to revive him. I always told him, "Work first, then snacks," but I broke my own rule almost every time. Life's too short to be stingy with the snacks.

He had been Connie's very first horse as a girl, and we had both been devastated by his death. And now, here we were again, stunned by the death of yet another resident. It was just too much for a heart to take.

When I got to the barn, I asked Wendy what had happened. She told me that Cricket had walked out into the arena, laid down, and in less than 20 seconds, had died. She'd been feeling poorly, not wanting to eat much. Wendy said that, whatever had been wrong with her, she hadn't suffered much in the way of pain: Wendy had dosed her fairly heavily with painkillers. She gestured to where Cricket lay in the arena and said, "Go be with her." Of all the humans I know, Wendy is one of the few who understand the need to spend some time with the animal's body, saying one's good-byes.

I sat down next to Cricket's head. I was still in evening attire and the thought raced briefly through my mind that I must look rather silly, all dressed up and sitting in urine-soaked sawdust. It didn't matter, of course; I would have made this same final visit in haute couture if that's what it took. While I sat there, my ears began to ring from the unnatural quiet. The horses seemed to know that this was not the time to be boisterous.

I stared down at Cricket for a long time, trying to take in the enormity of the loss.

I rubbed her face as I cried, sending out into the universe the twin thoughts that I would love her – and miss her – forever, and hoping that she heard them. And, because she was no longer there to stop me, I did the one thing in death that she never let me do in life: I stroked her big, fuzzy, rabbity ears. She had always pulled away when I reached for them. Now, there was nothing she could do about it.

I sat with her for quite some time. When I was finally ready to leave, I sought out Wendy, who was topping off the horses' water buckets. I nodded my understanding as she said, "I didn't sign on for this! I'm here to rescue them, not bury them!" I remarked to her the irony in my decision, made months before, to make it a "donkey Christmas" for the volunteers: each would, during our barn gift exchange, receive from me a framed picture of him or her standing next to Cricket. The pictures had been taken over a period of many months, on the rare occasions that the donkey had stood still long enough for me to get the shot. There was no way that any of us could have known that Cricket's time with us would be so limited. The "donkey Christmas" idea turned out to be a sad irony indeed.

The barn seemed extra quiet after that, without Cricket's unique braying. It was never much of a "hee haw," but rather more of a "chuff chuff chuff eeek-HAW!" I will especially miss the way she liked to keep me company when I cleaned stalls. She would come into the stall with me, and then proceed to block as much of the doorway as possible. She did this to all the volunteers, and they could frequently be heard complaining, "*Move*, Cricket!" Wendy dealt with the intrusions by threatening to put her in a stall out of the way of the workers if she didn't vacate the area voluntarily, but I always enjoyed Cricket's presence, and simply chose to work around her. If I couldn't get past her, I'd just stand there and scratch her back for a while. Cricket lived life on her own terms, and I saw no reason to insist that she do otherwise.

Connie, Wendy and I weren't the only ones grieving the loss of Cricket. Word spread fast among the volunteers via Facebook, and every one of them turned up noticeably subdued the following Saturday. "This sucks," texted Mandy after I'd relayed the news, "I totally loved her!!" Indeed, we'd all invested a large amount of time and energy in Cricket's care, over the years, and it felt as though she had taken a piece of each of us with her when she died. But then, isn't that always the way it feels when you lose a beloved pet?

LIFE LESSONS FROM GRANDPA WALTON

If you've been to my blog site, you'll know that I have little use for cable t.v. In the first place, I don't want to pay for it, and in the second, I don't want to spend that much time in front of the boob tube when I could be doing other things. When analog went the way of the dodo bird, I bought one of those digital converter boxes. It did its job well for about a year, and then suddenly, I couldn't tune in to any of Whoville's local channels anymore.

Initially, I thought the converter box had died, but that turned out not to be the case. I never did figure out what the problem was, but I have a sneaking suspicion that the cable company jammed the signal so that I'd be forced to pay for cable. It was the last thing I wanted to do but I didn't feel I could live without my weekly dose of *Grey's Anatomy,* so I signed up for the cheapest possible cable package.

It came as a surprise to learn that, as a cable subscriber, I was to get a few more channels that just my five network ones. Even so, I rarely gave them anything more than a glance until recently. Turns out the Hallmark channel shows reruns of several programs from my youth, like Little House on the Prairie, and The Walton's. I always liked those two!

Grandpa Walton was my favorite character. He was such a wise old soul, and his wisdom was always tempered with humor, and a willingness to indulge his grandchildren in a way that none of the other adults were inclined to do. Those other grown-ups always insisted that the kids behave and mind their manners. Grandpa, on the other hand, would merely grin and wink, knowing that sometimes, kids just need to be kids.

I generally have better things to do than watch a lot of t.v. But I'd run out of busy work, that day, and the nightly news wasn't on yet. I settled myself, more or less, to watching The Walton's until it was time to watch something more substantial.

I confess I was a little distracted. I had some other business on my mind, and kept tuning in and out mentally, as one does, catching a few lines of dialog and then wandering somewhere else in my head. At some point, though, it became clear that this wasn't just any old episode, and that I might get something out of it after all, if I paid attention.

It was an episode in which middle daughter Erin finds a lost fawn. She brings it home and insists on keeping it, even though her parents tell her no. At some point, the local park ranger (and who knew that Walton's Mountain had one of those?) turns up and tells Erin that it's illegal to keep a wild animal. As kindly as he can, for he understands that Erin's very upset about it, the ranger takes possession of the fawn and releases the little fellow back into the wild, where he's meant to be.

That's not the end of it, of course. That very night, Erin has a premonition that something bad is about to befall the fawn, and she convinces her father to help her go looking for it. Bringing the ranger along, Daddy Walton indulges his daughter, and all three proceed to search for the critter that Erin's named Lance.

The search party finds Lance just as shots ring out: the ranger's been having trouble with poachers on Walton's Mountain, and wouldn't you know, the poachers had taken aim at Lance. Fortunately, the fawn is found with little more than a flesh wound, and they bring him back to the Walton's barn for rest and rehab. The ranger tells Erin he knows about a fenced-in farm where he can take Lance. The deer would be safe behind that fence, he tells the child, and Erin can come and visit any time she likes. It sounds like the perfect solution.

That evening, as Erin fusses over Lance, Grandpa comes into the barn to give the deer some hay. Erin tells him about the fenced-in farm, and how happy she is that Lance will go somewhere safe. She asks Grandpa what he thinks about it, and he tells her, very gently, that he reckons that wild animals should be allowed to live wild. "Even though they'd be in danger?" she asks him. "Even so," says Grandpa. Living wild, he explains, means that Lance can run free, choose his own mate, and eat all the tender green grass he wants to. He might not be safe, but he'd be *free*.

And therein lies the crux: I awoke that morning to find a voice mail from Pat Mitchell on my answering machine. She had been at McKinnon's Pond and found Pretty Boy Duck's lifeless body at water's edge. She went on to say that her husband Pete had wrapped his body in a plastic bag and brought him back to their house. The body was waiting for me if I wanted to come and get it. Most folks wouldn't bother. I'm grateful that they did. As I made my way to their house, I held out a tiny hope that she was wrong, that it wasn't Pretty Boy after all, but another black duck at the pond, Baby Fuzz. Deep down, though, I knew that she knew exactly who that duck in the bag was.

As always happens when one of the ducks disappears, I agonized over the fact that I could've/should've found homes for them, safe homes with fences and people who understand about predators. At the same time, I can't help thinking what a (usually) wonderful place McKinnon's Pond is for a duck: it's *huge*, with plenty of territory for everyone, lots of mud for dabbling in, and a sense of freedom that I assume they enjoy. No one I know could possibly offer them anything remotely similar.

It's a quandary that I've dealt with for a number of years: find them safe, contained homes (and it must be said that those are in very short supply), or allow them to remain at the pond, at the mercy of various predators, and hope like hell that everything turns out o.k. It's not exactly a recipe for longevity. So it's striking that of all the Walton's episodes they could've shown that day, and of all the days I might've tuned in to watch, the episode I see has Grandpa Walton telling me that wild animals want to be wild.

I know that domestic ducks aren't wild animals, even though my gang is living wild. I know that they're meant to live on farms because that's what I keep telling the residents of Whoville, every time I write a letter to the paper asking them not to put live ducklings in their children's

Easter baskets. I *know*, for heaven's sake! I just have trouble getting past the fact that they have a huge pond at their disposal, and mates to keep them company, and that even though they seem glad to see me when I show up, every last one of them turns and walks away when our visit is over.

That doesn't make losing them any easier. As I listened to Grandpa Walton's words of wisdom that day, I burst into tears for Pretty Boy — a gregarious duck who never saw a pile of corn he didn't like. I cried again as I wrote this chapter, because I can never quite settle my mind to one thing or the other: safe, fenced-in ducks, or free but dicey? I wish I knew for sure.

It's worth noting that Pretty Boy was more than just some random duck. Indeed, he had a personality the size of Texas. That last time he was in my care, I learned quite a bit about him as we drove back and forth to various vet appointments. It turned out that he was a George Harrison fan, albeit a fairly picky one. I discovered this when I played my *Best of George Harrison* CD during one of those car rides. As the opening notes of "My Sweet Lord" began, Pretty Boy stopped scrabbling around on the hard plastic of the critter carrier, settled down on his stomach, and listened quietly. It was the first time he'd ever shut up while in my car!

I tried to turn him on to some other George Harrison tunes — most notably, "Here Comes the Sun," but he was having none of it. He rose to his feet again and resumed his escape attempt in earnest. "But Pretty Boy," I argued, "it's 'Here Comes the Sun'! That's a classic! Everyone loves it!" He conveyed his distaste by ignoring me completely.

Autistic author Temple Grandin mentions a number of research studies that suggest that animals communicate through music. Dogs, it's noted, will change the pitch and tone of their barks, depending on what the situation warrants.

There are also theories that humans didn't invent music after all, but copied what they heard various birds singing. Grandin sites an example where Mozart himself was influenced by a pet starling who re-wrote one of Mozart's concertos by changing the sharp notes to flat ones. Evidently, Amadeus preferred the bird's version of the song.

So it seemed only fitting for me to play "My Sweet Lord" in the car as I drove first to the Mitchell's to collect the body (crying all the way there), then as I headed to McKinnon's Pond (crying all the way there) for one last I-don't-know-what. It just seemed the thing to do, to take the body to the pond one last time. Then I drove him to his original vet's (crying all the way there) to drop him off for cremation. Dr. Chrys – the vet who amputated his cancerous wing – has been out of the country for some time, now, but she was still quite shocked about Pretty Boy's death when I emailed her later in the day. The staff at the animal hospital were equally subdued.

Feeling numb for most of the day helped take the edge off my raw nerves. I spent the day wishing it had all been a nightmare, and knowing that it hadn't been. By the time Grandpa Walton shared his critter philosophy with Erin, the floodgates opened and I sobbed for thirty minutes straight.

In the days that followed, I avoided "My Sweet Lord" and listened to "What is Life" instead. But that only made things worse: *Tell me, who am I without you by my side?* Who, indeed. Who was I, now that my *cause celebre* – the world-famous one-winged duck, my pal, the only duck who had ever made me laugh, the one I'd gladly shared a bathroom with – was gone? There were still twelve ducks at the pond that needed me. But the only one I'd developed a deep, trusting bond with was Pretty Boy.

Because the Gods seem to prefer balance in the universe, a thing happened a week or so later that offered a much-needed reminder that life does go on, and that other critters do need me. I was driving through Whoville when I passed Animal Control Officer Dave standing half-way down a ditch. Owing to the rain we had recently, there was a fair amount of water running through it. I passed on by thinking that whatever he was up to, I probably didn't want to know about it. It was most likely some horribly mangled dead critter, and I just didn't want to deal with it.

So I kept driving. And kept telling myself to go back and help him out. I managed to get about half a mile down the road before I impulsively turned into a driveway, backed up, and returned the way I'd come. I pulled off the road, crossed the street and hollered, "Need a hand?" The noise of passing traffic whittled his answer down to "dog" and "blind."

The dog in question – a yellow lab – seemed to be walking with some purpose in the water. When he headed for a culvert, I saw my opportunity and jogged to the other end of the pipe, making my way down to water's edge as he reappeared. He turned his head to me when I called him, and it was then that I saw what Officer Dave was talking about: two milky white orbs stared sightlessly in my direction.

I began calling loudly, then, and clapping my hands. The dog walked right up to me, and I held him fast with one hand while I gave him some rubs with the other. "Good boy," I told him, "what a good boy you are!" Dave walked up then and handed me a leash. I looped it over the dog's head and handed the dog off to him. As we headed back to our respective vehicles, speculating on why a blind dog was out roaming around all alone without a tag or collar, Dave announced, "People are really dumb sometimes!" Yes, Dave, they sure are.

As I drove off down the road again, it hit me how ironic that rescue had been: there was the perfectly able and experienced Animal Control Officer, having trouble catching a dog. And then the Critter Lady happens on the scene and snags the dog on the first try. Sometimes, life just happens like that, and the folks around me remark, "Wow! How 'bout that?!" And I usually say the obvious in response, "Well, I *am* the Critter Lady..." Although I would continue to struggle over the issue of domestic ducks living wild, giving Officer Dave a hand was just the pick-me-up I'd needed to move past my funk over Pretty Boy's death.

As you might imagine, Erin chewed on Grandpa's words and realized that he was right. At the end of the show, she took Lance up on Walton's Mountain and released him. He hung around for a couple of minutes, and then dashed off into the woods, where he could live free.

What I loved best about Pretty Boy was his alpha-duck-ness, a striking assertiveness that I've seen in no other duck on the pond. He trusted me enough to let me pick him up, and then he asserted himself – every single time – and let me know that he had better things to do than to go somewhere with me. In spite of the untimely end to his life, I know that Pretty Boy had some good years at the pond: he was well-fed, he had a mate whose company he enjoyed, and he had a loving human who plied him with corn and looked after him as best she could. Sometimes, I can do no more than that.

Having plowed through the majority of my inheritance, I took a part-time job as a greeter at a family-owned department store not named Wal-Mart. The irony of having to be nice to the very humans I usually tried hard to avoid was not lost on me, and I found that the mental energy required to do my job well was exhausting. While my therapist hoped that the forced contact would improve my social skills a little, the job actually had the opposite effect: on my days off, I avoided people even more than I had before. Naturally, I turned to the critters around me for solace yet again.

MOUSE IN THE HOUSE

When I had lived at the chicken coop, I knew from the day I moved in that I would be sharing the place with more critters than just my cats: there was the chipmunk I'd seen coming and going via a hole in the roof, and there were the resident mice, as well. I knew about the mice because the cats would periodically position themselves in front of a small crack in the laundry room wall. I never minded those boarders, and if you've read *Crazy Critter Lady,* you'll know that I went to great pains to rescue as many mice as possible. Little did I know that the Critter Shack also came with uninvited guests.

My first encounter came when I climbed out of bed one morning to find Spanky and Buddy staring intently at a big wicker basket in the corner of my bedroom. It could only mean one thing: there was a mouse back there somewhere. Sure enough, when I peeked behind the basket, I saw a small brown mouse.

I'd known about him for quite some time, having found mouse poops in the knife drawer. You might think a mouse hanging out in a knife drawer is a little strange until I tell you that the cabinet where I keep the cat kibble is directly below that knife drawer! Apart from the occasional poops, though, I never saw the mouse himself. Indeed, so much time would pass between poops that I began to wonder if he'd moved out altogether. My cats knew better, though.

I know that many folks set traps, and shudder at the mere thought of a mouse invasion. Mice don't bother me, though. I figure they're God's creatures, too, and they all have a right to exist. As I see it, my job is to live and let live. Because my cats see things differently, I'm accustomed to running interference and rescuing rodents when I'm able. So instead of trying to eradicate the problem, I spent some time that morning trying to coax the mouse out from behind the wicker basket and into my closet.

This took some doing because mice don't generally understand that I'm a benevolent giant intent on saving their lives. They just think I'm big and scary-looking. After a few minutes spent watching the little guy ping-pong back and forth around the bedroom, I finally managed to shoo him into the closet. The last thing I saw before I shut the door was that tiny creature leaping into one of my shoes. I assumed I wouldn't see him again for a while. Naturally, I was wrong.

I was watching the nightly news later on that same day when I heard the mouse squeaking. There was a brief cranial delay before my brain realized that the noise meant he was back and the cats had found him. I hustled out of my chair and raced to the front room, where I found all four cats circling the room the way cats do when they're excited. I spotted the mouse behind the console, and spent some time trying to catch him. As usual, though, he managed to evade me and disappeared without a trace.

Before heading back to my chair and the news, I thought I'd make a pit stop in the bathroom. When I walked in, though, I realized that the mouse hadn't entirely disappeared; he'd managed to find a new hiding place behind the wicker shelves. Judging from Buddy's *I know you're there* position in front of the shelves, it was obvious that Buddy did, in fact, know that the mouse was there!

After chucking Buddy out of the bathroom and closing the door, I had to stop and think about my strategy. Those little field mice move fast, and I've lost more of them than I've actually caught over the years. I formulated a plan, and then left the room to put together the necessary tools. I grabbed a sieve from the kitchen, and a small sheet of cardboard from my office, and returned to the bathroom.

When I pulled the wicker shelves away from the wall, the hair dryer and curling iron that had been lying forgotten on top dropped like rocks to the floor. I winced, then, and hoped that the little guy hadn't been flattened by them. Glancing around the room, I spotted him desperately trying to squeeze himself between the grates of the heating vent. The grating was too narrow, though, so he raced off in search of another escape route. At some point, he accidentally cornered himself against the toilet. Now was my chance!

Waving at him with one hand, I held the sieve in the other, poised above him. The minute he ran in the direction I wanted him to go, down came the sieve. Gently, I slipped the sheet of cardboard underneath it, sandwiching the mouse in between. Now I had him. Once I caught him, though, I had to give some thought to what, exactly, I could do with him. Outside was an ice storm, with five-odd inches of snow still to come. It was much too cold out there to simply throw him out, knowing that he had no warm nest to go to. On the other hand, I couldn't just release him any old place in the house because those four cats of mine weren't the least bit interested in sharing their home!

When I drew on the knowledge I had of my lodger, the fact that he'd been able to stay hidden behind the walls for so long gave me pause for thought. I realized that if I could aim him in the direction of the interior walls of the house, he'd be o.k. So while the little fellow paced around under the sieve, I cleaned out the cupboard beneath my kitchen sink. There's a weird space back behind the shelf, where the indoor water meter resides. When I stuck my head in there for a look, I saw a tunnel, if you will, running behind the cupboard. I imagine that's how the mouse got around, using that space behind my kitchen cupboards. It was the perfect release site.

I held the sieve in one hand while my other supported the sheet of cardboard. Tilting the cardboard downward into that empty space, I lifted the sieve and watched as the mouse plopped down into the tunnel and ran off. Another successful rescue!

As I returned the cleaning supplies to their shelf, I watched in amusement as the cats circled the room, clearly confounded by the disappearance of the mouse. They're always perplexed at times like this, and they can't understand for the life of them why I feel compelled to ruin their fun. Our conversations go something like this:

Junebug: *Why can't we have him, Kelly?*
Kelly: "Because I like mice, that's why."
Junebug: *But Kelly! I like mice, too!*
Kelly: "Yes, but I like them when they're still alive and wiggly!"
Junebug: *Me, too, Kelly! I like wiggly mice, too!*
Kelly: "But I don't want to *eat* them, Little Mitten!"
Junebug: *I will eat them for you, Kelly!*
Kelly: "No, thanks, Junebug!"

A Little Bit of Beau

While I took several lessons on Charlie Horse, they turned out to be underwhelming endeavors. In the first place, his sour personality left no room for building a relationship, and in the second, his trot and lope were so pokey and slow that I might as well have been riding one of those one-cent mechanical horses they have out in front of stores. At thirty bucks a lesson, it just wasn't *fun* enough to keep trying.

It wasn't necessarily Charlie's fault. My understanding is that Charlie had been treated roughly before he came to the barn, rendering his mouth very sensitive. Riders had to be extremely careful to stay out of his mouth while they rode, and steer mainly with their legs. While that may sound like an easy thing to do, there's definitely an art to it, and it takes time to learn to finesse: I've seen a couple of the young volunteers give him what they thought was a command to step sideways, while Charlie thought it was the command to lope off. Two inexperienced youngsters got quite an unexpected ride that day!

But while Charlie's willing enough to tolerate having people on his back, he makes it very clear that he's not interested in bonding with us. Sadly, he doesn't seem to want much to do with humans, which takes all the fun out of riding him.

I began making dissatisfied noises to Wendy. There were over twenty other horses in residence at the barn; surely one of them would suit my needs. But although there were plenty to choose from, there were very few actual candidates: rescue Buddy had horrible issues stemming from a yearling halter that had been left on too long, so he would never let anyone put a bridle on him. Jem had conformation issues that rendered him unusable as anything other than a pasture pal. Newman's too old, and Magic, too young. Wendy *did* have an older rescue horse that needed to be ridden regularly, but Angel tended to be shy and skittish which, as it happens, are the two main reasons I preferred not to ride her. That just left Bit.

Little Bit of Beau was an EPM horse. EPM is a disease that affects the central nervous system. Symptoms can include tripping and loss of coordination – huge problems when you're trying to compete on a horse! I'm told that Bit displayed those symptoms before he came to The Harmony Barn, and had been treated for them upon arrival. EPM is not curable, but it *can* be managed. I don't think that EPM was the reason that Bit was never considered an option for us to ride, though. I think the reason had more to do with his personality.

I'll be honest here and say that I spent several years disliking Bit. He was much too in-your-face for me. If you stood next to him, he'd push his head against you and knock you off balance. While old Newman had ruled the herd with quiet authority, Bit, his protégé, rules with an iron hoof! Where old Newman would only have to walk into the arena for the horses to settle down, Bit feels the need to run around pinning his ears at everyone! He was way too much horse for me, so I didn't give him a second thought until Ruckus died, and Charlie proved unsatisfactory.

I posed the question to Wendy, asking what she thought about Connie giving me lessons on Bit. Much to my considerable surprise, she thought the idea had possibilities and the next thing I knew, Connie and I had scheduled a lesson. I anticipated that first lesson with more than a little trepidation.

Contrary to his name, there's nothing little about Bit. He's one big horse! Tall, muscular, assertive – at 16hh, he can be quite intimidating. I did my best to act nonchalant as I groomed him that first time, but inwardly, I was thinking about how far down the ground was going to be, should I end up getting tossed out of the saddle. I had seen a more experienced girl ride him, and there had been a lot of prancing on his part. What chance did I have as a novice who lacked confidence? Connie tried to reassure me, but I was skeptical. For his part, Bit gave me plenty to think about during – and after – that first lesson.

For one thing, if he didn't want to do what I told him, he'd do something else instead. The "something else" generally involved low-level shenanigans like prancing about (which, for the uninitiated, feels like the horse is about to take off at a gallop and leave you behind), and throwing in the odd buck and rear. These weren't full blown bucks and rears, but rather, just enough to emphasize his point. I lost track of how many times I frantically asked Connie, *"What's he doing? What's he doing?"* To her credit, Connie managed to stifle whatever chuckling she surely wanted to do. "You're o.k.," she kept saying, "he's not going to hurt you!" And in this, she turned out to be right.

In spite of my anxiety, I was intrigued enough to schedule another lesson on Bit – and another, and another! After several successful lessons, Connie expressed her belief that Bit and I were coming together as a team quite nicely. I was inclined to agree: while he continued to throw his own brand of challenges into every lesson, we *did* find ways to communicate together that told me we were on the right track. Indeed, the most telling communication of all didn't even happen during a lesson. It happened one day after the volunteers had finished mucking out stalls.

Being the Critter Lady, I take a lot of pictures at the barn. I take pictures of all the kids with their favorite horses, and I have them take pictures of me with mine. Anyone who follows me on Facebook knows that Bit rarely stands still for pictures. Don't get me wrong, he stands still just fine, until you aim a camera at him! Then he's all about swinging his huge head around, and trying to use me as a scratching post. But on that day, he stood still for a number of pictures with me, and even some with the kids as well. When we were done, I unhooked the lead rope and told him he was free to go boss the herd around. But here's the thing: he didn't leave.

While I took pictures of Lydia and Buddy, and Michaela and Angel, there was Bit, lurking about. While I took pictures of Allen and Charlie, there was Bit, lurking about. He stood here for a time, then moved a few feet away and stood there for a time, all the while looking over at me to see whether I had a snack for him, or possibly a command or two. The striking thing was that he was looking *to* me – for direction, for companionship – rather than looking *at* me, and this was the first time he'd ever done that on his own. It was a satisfying moment indeed when I realized that.

There can be a world of difference between what goes on on a horse's back, and what goes on in the mud lot, where he's free to do as he pleases. When Charlie Horse is under saddle, he behaves pretty well. When he's in the mud lot, he'd just as soon stand off by himself and crib, rather than interact with us humans. Similarly, Bit's usually too busy moving the herd from one side of the poop pile to the other and back to take notice of what the volunteers are up to. Ordinarily, he would give us all a cursory glance, make sure we weren't doing anything that required his attention, and then go on about his business. To hang around with me for twenty-odd minutes of his own volition was extraordinary!

There's definitely a relationship forming between Bit and I, and there's much more to it than just getting on his back and riding. The time I spend with him on the ground is also an investment in the bond that's developing, and it's just what I'd been needing after suffering the loss of Ruckus. There will never be a replacement horse: there was, and ever will be, only one Ruckus. But as I've observed before, it *is* necessary to move forward, to form new relationships with other critters, to let yourself love again, even though you *know* that one day, your heart will be broken by yet another critter death. These wonderful relationships are vital to the well-being of our souls, and quite possibly theirs, too. They're what make life worth living.

THE GREAT
CRAYFISH RESCUE

While the vast majority of my rescues involve warm-blooded animals, there *are* occasions when some other kind of creature is in need: in the summer, I'll relocate the praying mantises who are in danger of being mowed; in the fall, I'll move snakes off the park trail. While I'm not a huge fan of bugs, I try to do my part and show them some compassion. Such was the case one day when I was out walking around my neighborhood.

It's a neighborhood full of brick ranch houses, and I'm always a little baffled as to the need for such housing conformity. The way I see it, the builder of those homes either lacked the finances to build a broader array of housing styles, or lacked the imagination to think them up. Either way, the neighborhood is pretty homogenous – and monotonous – and I usually drive a few miles up the road to one of the area's metroparks to do my walking. On this particular day, though, I was feeling lazy and didn't want to make the drive. So I settled for a walk around the ranch houses instead.

My mind was wandering as I walked. It was a beautiful day out, with the sun shining brightly, and the temperature nice and mild. We'd had quite a bit of rain recently so the sunshine was particularly welcome. I was daydreaming as I walked, not thinking about anything special, so I almost missed the fact that a leaf was walking toward me. When it nicked the corner of my gaze, I stopped to get a better look.

While I wear glasses, and the prescription is up to date, wires sometimes get crossed in my head and don't translate things properly: the "leaf" that I initially saw walking toward me wasn't a leaf at all but rather a very large crayfish! I haven't seen one of those since I was a kid!

You can imagine my surprise. How on earth did a water-critter end up on the pavement a good mile away from the nearest creek? Turning the matter over in my head, I surmised that he'd been tossed up through a storm grate by those heavy rains we'd had recently. It was the most likely explanation.

He looked an awful lot like a spider with all those legs. And I hate spiders! But there was no question of leaving him in the street to be run over. Moving him into someone's yard didn't seem to fit the bill, either. He belonged near a creek, and there just happened to be one running through the property behind my house. Gingerly, I picked the critter up and set him in the palm of my hand. He remained there, immobile, for so long that I thought I'd killed him. Turned out he was just taking stock of his new situation.

I wasn't terribly keen to cut my walk short, so I kept going, crayfish in tow. I must've looked ridiculous, walking down the street staring at my open hand! When I rounded the last corner, changing direction just enough for the sun to shine down on the newly christened "Buddy," the crayfish seemed to wake up. Now he wanted to walk, too, and I had to keep putting one hand in front of the other as he walked across them in an earnest attempt to escape.

I made a quick stop at my house to grab the camera: I wanted some proof that this rescue really happened because I was fairly certain that even the people who knew me wouldn't believe me. I put Buddy in a bowl that he couldn't crawl out of, took a few snaps, then made my way to the creek.

Owing to all the precipitation we'd had recently, the creek was moving fast and high. I entertained more than a few passing thoughts about the possibility of my falling in and being swept away, and concluded that I really didn't want to go swimming that day. Sometimes, I question my own sanity: I *did* have a tendency to put myself in iffy situations for critters in need. I hoped that this wouldn't be one of them.

When I told this story to Mandy later out at the barn, she teasingly asked me whether I'd weighed the crayfish's new home site options, or just tossed him down any old place. It must be said that Mandy relishes every opportunity she can find to zing me, and I handed her this one on a silver platter. I mean, of *course* I chose his new home site carefully! Hell, I spent a good ten minutes in a lather of indecision over placing him on one side of the bridge – which consisted mainly of broken chunks of concrete, and the other side of the bridge – which was mostly twigs and the usual detritus you find creek- side.

Twigs and detritus are, of course, preferable to chunks of concrete. But there was a hitch: the twiggy area could only be got to by first passing through a couple of shrubs with branches full of thorns longer than my fingers! Once I made it past that obstacle, then there was the loose earth to worry about: I wasn't sure whether I was actually standing on solid ground, or just a bunch of sticks that were floating at water's edge.

I know what you're thinking. "Jeez, Kelly, all this fuss over a crayfish? Why bother?" My answer is, "Why *not* bother?" Where do you draw the line and stop helping? It's o.k. to help dogs and cats, but the crayfish of the world are on their own? I swear to you that I don't go looking for these things, but there he was, a critter in need, so I stepped up to the plate and helped. He most surely would've died otherwise, and I didn't want that on my conscience.

So I trod very carefully on the sticks and twigs. I chose a spot where he could rest and take stock first, and then hop in the water when he was ready. I picked him up out of the bowl and gently set him down. Then I crouched there, waiting, to make sure he knew what to do. After considerable assessment on his part, Buddy slowly made his way across the sticks until he found a place he felt comfortable with. Watching for a few more minutes while nothing happened, I concluded that he was indeed where he wanted to be, and I carefully made my way back through the obstacle course. Heading home, I basked in a small glow of satisfaction that I had helped a critter that no one else would have even noticed, and asked a small prayer of the Gods that they look after the little fellow in my absence.

As I stood on a balcony on December 31st, 1999, watching the neighbor's fireworks display, I had a premonition that the new millennium would bring great change. I had no evidence to support this thought, nor any reason to believe that it might actually be true. Indeed, the next thirteen-odd years were not great ones: there were financial hardships, ongoing struggles with mental illness, and dysfunctional relationships with men who were not worthy of me. Eventually, though, thanks to years of therapy with the right counselor, life slowly began to sort itself out, and the Gods threw me a happy curveball that I never expected to see.

DUDLEY

His name is Dudley, but no one ever called him that. To those of us who shared the small town of Whoville with him, he was "Duddy." He first turned up on my radar in junior high school, when I heard girls talking about him. Cute, slender, with a mop of sun-bleached hair and an easy-going nature, all the girls wanted to date him. He was a year younger than I, though, so I didn't give him much thought until I saw him at a party a couple of years into high school.

Those high school parties were all about under-age drinking. Any time someone's parents went out of town, we gathered in large numbers, bringing with us illicitly-bought booze, bongs, and whatever else we could get our hands on. We'd turn the music up loud enough to piss off the neighbors, and generally have a fine time pickling our livers while Whoville's Finest turned a blind eye to our antics: many of the heaviest drinkers were star players on the high school sports teams.

This particular party was the same as all the others but for one thing: Duddy was there, and he had with him an acoustic guitar. He and his buddy Jeff sat down a few feet away from me and proceeded to play a surprising repertoire: songs by America, and Neil Young, played well and with feeling. One of the two young musicians – I can no longer recall who – even played harmonica, as well.

Of the little that I actually do remember about my time in high school, 30-odd years later, I remember this: Duddy played America's "Lonely People" and it was magical. It was magical because for the two minutes and twenty-seven seconds that it took him to play the song, Duddy was lost in the music, and I, lost in him, watching. I was fascinated! He seemed so comfortable in his own skin, so confident. And so cute!

A year or so later, I worked up the courage to ask him to accompany me to one of Whoville High's formal dances. To my everlasting surprise, he said yes. While I have no memories of the dance itself, I vividly recall how, as we stood in front of the fireplace at his mom's house posing for pictures, he leaned over and kissed me on the cheek. I was instantly transported to a heaven that I didn't know existed! It seemed so important then, and so silly now, but that impulsive peck cemented Duddy's place in my memory. To this day, I feel the same giddiness, recalling the moment, that I felt at the time it happened.

There were a few make-out sessions after that dance, but we were never a couple. I don't know why. We drifted through the subsequent years of high school running around with our respective crowds, and then I joined the service. While I didn't stay in for the entire period of enlistment, I was still in the army when Duddy's younger sister Katharine – who I had befriended my junior year for the admittedly selfish reason of wanting to spend more time in Duddy's orbit – sent me a picture with a note attached: Duddy had gotten married. At nineteen! She was a local girl, and they were expecting. Our lives took wildly divergent paths, then. But while I wouldn't see Duddy again for many years, I never forgot him entirely.

He came back on the radar just after his mother died, some eighteen years later. I read the obituary in the *Whoville Journal* and immediately got in touch with Katharine. She and I spent a few months, then, keeping each other company as she worked through her grief. Newly divorced, Duddy was playing some gigs with a band at a local bar, and we'd go watch them play. It was fun, but it wasn't magical — there were too many people there, and it was too impersonal. The magic happened when Duddy came by his sister's house one evening and stayed into the small hours of the night.

Pulling out the guitar he'd brought with him, he stood before me and serenaded me with America's "Lonely People." I sat on the couch in awe, feeling like a shy teenager all over again. For a while, time stood still, and we were cocooned in a moment that neither of us wanted to end. He was at a place in his life that wouldn't permit him to take things any further than those few precious minutes. I mustered my courage anyway and let him know I was open to the idea of dating him, if things didn't work out with the current girl. The comment floated between us but nothing else was said. At the time, I took Duddy's silence to mean he wasn't interested. It would be twelve years before I learned that I couldn't have been more wrong.

Those twelve years were hard ones for Duddy, and for me. I spent them dealing with the aftermath of having been molested as a child, suffering from depression, isolation, and Post Traumatic Stress Disorder. Slowly, as time went by, I found a measure of self, and sanity. At the same time, Duddy's life spiraled out of control. There was a hideously toxic relationship, drinking and drugs. I had no idea how awful things were until I found Katharine on Facebook and asked my usual *how's Duddy these days?* The answer shocked me, and I fully expected to hear that Duddy had died from alcoholism, or something worse. I actually spent some time listening to my *Best of America* CD and thinking about what I might say at his funeral. It was that bad.

You can imagine my surprise when he turned up on Facebook, alive and well! I immediately sent a friend request, which was granted within minutes. We got to messaging, then, me asking questions, and Duddy responding with mostly monosyllabic answers:

"How are you doing these days?"

"Gettin' old."

"Playing much?"

"No band now, just me." I was getting nowhere fast when I threw out the game-changer: "What's a girl got to do to get you to play for her?" That did the trick! Next thing I knew, I was picking him up at the sober-living house where he stayed, and driving to Olive Garden, where I spent the next few hours being pleasantly surprised.

He peered at me over the glasses that had slipped down his nose. It was an incredibly endearing look, made all the more so by his determination to tell me his story. The words spilled out, tumbling on top of one another in his hurry to fill me in. Yes, he said, there had been years of chaos and insanity. After his marriage ended, there was a relationship in which he had become a battered boyfriend, and alcoholism that would've killed him if it had gone on any longer. The transitional house was his salvation, coming, as it did, after thirty days of inpatient rehab. Duddy was sober, and proud of it. His new-found enthusiasm for life was infectious, and by the end of the evening, I found myself hoping that we would see each other again soon.

In fact, we got together again the very next night. He brought his guitar along, and spent an hour or so singing all sorts of songs — including "Lonely People." It was my own private concert, and I relished every minute of it. Things had clearly changed between us, after all those years, but the changes were for the better: now, we brought sanity and sobriety to the mix, as well as the maturity that comes from having lived and learned. We were still giddy teenagers, but we were sensible adults now, too. It was an interesting mix of feelings.

When the radio announced that America would be playing a concert near us later that spring, we jumped at the chance to see them. We arrived early at the gated community that was hosting the gig, marveling at the genteel charm of the village as well as the incredibly cheap ticket prices. The seats in the 80 year-old auditorium were first come-first serve. We ended up in row 17, center aisle. We couldn't have bought better seats at any other venue. When America came on stage and started singing "Lonely People," things seemed to come full circle: there I was, listening to the band whose songs Duddy had played at that party all those years ago, and there he was, sitting right next to me, playing air guitar to his favorite tunes. It was – yep, you guessed it! – *magical!*

It was unfortunate that Gerry Beckley had some sort of voice issue going on that rendered him more of a Muppet than an actual singer. Imagine Kermit the frog singing "A Horse With No Name" and you'll understand what I mean. His backup vocals were fine, but when he sang lead, his voice went places it simply shouldn't have, which sent Duddy and I into fits of giggles. And here's the thing: Duddy and I laugh with abandon. We giggle like teenagers. And we smile like people who have been to hell and back and are grateful to have survived the trip. Life is suddenly *very* interesting indeed!

We knew immediately that we wanted to be together, that the time had finally come for us to see what we could make of it. Within a few months of our initial contact on Facebook, Dud had moved into the Critter Shack and we settled happily into the relationship that we'd been wondering about all those years. It was not without its difficulties: apart from anything else, I suffer from more than one mental illness, and Dud had his own messes from the past to clean up. Alcoholics tend to leave a lot of relationships in their wake, family members who bear the brunt of years of neglect. All of those matters would need to be addressed many times before wounded hearts could mend, but we faced them together, with the certainty that comes from finally knowing where and with whom you belong. Within a month of moving in, Dud proposed and I said yes. At long last, the Gods saw fit to reward all my years of misery and struggle.

Six Pekins

As if people dumping domestic ducks on a semi-regular basis weren't enough, I got word in early summer that someone had abandoned six Pekins at the nameless little pond just up the street from McKinnon's. I'm told that someone witnessed a child leaving the ducks, but six full-grown Pekins is more than one youngster could handle; there's no doubt in my mind that at least one adult was also involved. When I went to check them out for myself, I thought tiredly that I didn't have the energy to worry about six more ducks, and I wondered what could be done about them.

One of my duck-feeding volunteers and I both attempted to get close to the Pekins by offering them food, but they were terrified of everything and everyone. They hadn't even gone in the pond, yet – a thing I would eventually use to my advantage when it came time to rescue them. I had no idea whether they had eaten recently or not, but they weren't eating what Liz and I left for them. Clearly, they needed rescuing as soon as possible. Naturally, my first call was to Officer Dave. "You're not going to believe this one," I told him. "I was just going to call you," he replied, already knowing what my call was about. We agreed to meet in the pond parking lot to form a strategy.

While I felt optimistic about our chances of catching the ducks, I had no idea what to do with them once they were in our possession. Finding someone who wanted a pet duck was about as easy as finding a needle in a haystack. Fortunately, Officer Dave had a place all lined up – *if* we could catch them. Enigmatically, he refused to tell me the name of the ducks' benefactor, but when he mentioned that the place was a farm out in the country, I breathed a sigh of relief; it was a rare day in the neighborhood when we had a place to take our rescues, let alone a *farm*.

Dave and I walked out toward the pond, staying well away from the frightened ducks. I told him I thought we needed a staging area, something fenced to herd them into, and some warm bodies to do the herding. Dave said he could take care of all that; working for the City of Whoville has its' advantages: Dave borrowed some temporary orange plastic fencing from the Streets Department, and some teenagers from the Summer Employment Program. I had wanted a day or two to finalize our plan, but Dave was due to start his vacation the very next day and wanted to get the rescue taken care of beforehand. "Today?" I mused skeptically.

"Today!" he said firmly, "after I take my lunch break."

"O.k.," I sighed in resignation, "I'll meet you back here in an hour."

We had a huddle with the four teenagers Dave had rounded up. I explained that we would fan out in a semi-circle, walking very slowly toward the ducks, who remained huddled near a tree. I would try to herd them away from the water and toward the fencing that Dave and I had set up before he went to lunch. "It won't take much movement on our part to herd them," I told the kids, "we'll look like giants to them anyway, so no waving your arms above your heads. Just walk slowly and move your hands a little. Once we get them into the fence, come on up and close it around us." Dave had brought a large cage to put them in. We left it near his truck for the time being.

We got into position, and I gave the signal to begin. Slowly, we all moved forward. The closer we got to the Pekins, the more nervous they became until eventually, they started walking away from us *en masse*. If any of the teenagers started walking too quickly, I would gently wave them back before advancing again at the snail's pace that seemed to be working. I could hear the ducks clucking softly to each other, clearly wondering what was going on, and what they should do about it. No one among the humans spoke. Closer and closer we got to the fencing. The operation was going much more smoothly than I had anticipated. As long as the ducks didn't veer off into the pond at the last minute! If that happened, we would be sunk, and there would be no way to catch them.

We continued our slow but steady advance. The ducks continued their slow but steady retreat. Finally, amazingly, they walked right into the semi-circle of fencing and then stood against it, uncertain what to do next. "Bring that fencing around!" I told the kids. As the fence closed around us, Dave and I gave each other a look, and I knew exactly what he was thinking: *boy, did we get lucky!* The kids handed the cage to us over the fence and Dave set it on end, thinking we would drop them down into it. I looked at him askance, then: duck legs are *very* breakable, and we would break more than one leg if we dropped the ducks down into the cage. I turned the thing over on its side and told Dave to man the gate: I would take on the task of catching the six Pekins.

While the ducks didn't actually stand still and make catching them easy, they made it easy *enough*. One by one, I would chase them down and corner them against the fence, then pick them up and deposit them firmly in the cage. Rounding them all up took less than five minutes, and once they'd all been caught, I insisted on getting a few pictures for posterity. It wasn't every day – or indeed, *ever* – that six Pekins got dumped, let alone rescued, in Whoville. As Dave loaded the cage into the back of his City crittering truck, I told him to thank the anonymous benefactor for me.

We got lucky. We got *very* lucky. Considering the fact that at the same time we were helping the six Pekins, there were twelve domestic ducks still living rough just up the street at McKinnon's pond because they weren't particularly catchable, and because no one wanted them, we marveled at how easy it had been to catch the six ducks and find them a home.

Officer Dave and I were mighty pleased with ourselves over this one: being in the rescue business means we both have had our share of successes, and we've had our share of failures. We never have enough of the former, and we always have too many of the latter. A good day's work was always immensely satisfying, and I could tell that Dave was particularly pleased because he'd put his faith in me yet again, and it had paid off yet again. Indeed, we were so elated that we shared not one, but two congratulatory fist bumps! We parted company hoping we wouldn't be called upon to do any more rescues like that one any time soon.

Tolerating the Occasional Human

(Part Two)

If the idea of a person who suffers from depression taking a job in which her entire shift requires her to interact with other human beings seems odd to you, I can assure you that the incongruity was not lost on me, either. Every single time I walked out onto the floor, I had to consciously flip a mental switch to turn my personality on. It was not an easy thing to do. In the first place, I've spent the majority of my life being painfully shy, and in the second place, more loopy people walked through the doors of that store than I thought was possible, and they frequently left me standing in their wake with my mouth wide open.

At first I thought the main reason for all the loopiness had to do with the part of town my branch of Maytag's was located in: the east side of Whoville is *not* an affluent area by any means. Indeed, I suspect that more welfare recipients frequented that branch of the store than any of the others. But it wasn't necessarily the poor folks who had me shaking my head; the middle-class ones were often the most outrageous of all. Either way, though, whether poor or of comfortable means, the great number of curious characters who frequented Maytag's never failed to amaze me.

There was Fred, who was, hands down, *the* most boring person on the entire planet. Every time he walked into the store, he made a beeline for me and proceeded to spend the next twenty minutes regaling me with such dull stories of his life that I had trouble stifling my yawns. The only good thing about those conversations was that they killed twenty minutes of my shift. The poor guy meant well, he just had no clue how incredibly boring he was.

There was Scruffy Security Guard Guy. Scruffy came in to shop just about every day. He always wore the same rumpled security guard uniform. What I didn't know until LP (Loss Prevention, with whom the greeters were closely affiliated) told me was that they'd caught him shoplifting at another Maytag's location. Evidently, he'd been so traumatized by getting caught that he'd shed big remorseful tears and begged them not to tell his boss, as he'd surely lose his job. I'm certain that the irony was lost on him, but it left me shaking my head in astonishment: *A security guard? Shoplifting?!*

There was Pearl Wittering, who kept running for Mayor of Whoville no matter how few votes she got. Campaigning on what was apparently the Crazier Than Your Average Citizen ticket, she drove around all year long with a huge "Vote for Pearl!" sign on top of her car. It's a wonder the thing never got caught on low-hanging overpasses. She was the laughingstock of the local mainstream politicians; no one took her seriously. She only ever garnered a few hundred votes, but her optimism never dimmed: during one of our chats, she raised her fist high above her bouffant hairdo and exclaimed, "This is going to be the year! I can feel it!"

There was the toothless old fellow with the tracheotomy who always used a motorized cart to get around the store. I never did find out why he had a hole in his throat, but he always had a wave for me, and when I'd ask, "How ya doin', Sweetheart?" he'd cover the hole and give me a cheery answer.

There was Spongebob Squarepants Lady. A wizened little black woman who looked older than she really was, Squarepants would come in wearing the same filthy clothes every single time: a dirty orange hooded sweatshirt – with the hood always in the upright position, as though she believed that if she couldn't see you from under that hood, then you couldn't see her, either; dirty fleece pants with Spongebob all over them; and a ragged pair of shoes. She wore this same outfit year-round. When I called LP and asked whether we were watching Squarepants, the answer I got was, "No, the only thing she ever steals is the toilet paper in the bathroom." We assumed that she was homeless. She never uttered a word to any of us, ever.

There was Rudy. A delightful older Hispanic fellow, I always greeted him in enthusiastic *Cheers!* fashion by hollering, "Rudy!" as he walked in the door. Rudy came in just about every day for a newspaper and a lottery ticket. It was well known that Rudy had won over $30,000 playing the lottery. Curiously, he never spent so much as a penny of his winnings filling the vacancies in his mouth: Rudy's poor dentistry was typical of many East Side folks – women as well as men.

There was the old woman who, upon discovering that there were no small shopping carts available and that she would have to make do with a regular-sized one, stomped her foot in anger and announced, "I *won't* shop without a small cart!" I could do no more than stare in astonishment at her outburst. The next time she came in, she stood in front of me, looking pointedly first to my left, then to my right. I stepped out of the way and with a sweep of my arm toward the cart corral said, "Ma'am, I assure you that I am *not* hiding the small carts behind me!" She walked off in a huff.

There was Frank, the desperately lonely, overweight, middle-aged Italian guy who couldn't get a date no matter how hard he tried. I got a kick out of talking to Frank because he was so personable, and he always made me laugh. More than once, he threatened to sweep me off my feet and take me somewhere exotic. I would flash my engagement ring at him and say, "Sorry, Francis, you're a day late and a dollar short!" Bemused, he would reply that that was the story of his life.

If Maytag's customers were loopy, the staff were even more so. There was Terry the cashier, who, for whatever reason, dyed his long brown hair blonde. He took a fancy to the color and left it that way, eventually deciding that it brought good luck to his darts team. He kept bleaching the roots throughout the tournament, but when his team lost, Terry's wife made him cut it all off. Having done so, he dyed the new shorter hair a rusty orange hue. It was his quiet way of thumbing his nose at conformity.

There was the enormous grocery girl – and when I say enormous, I mean that she was so fat that it hurt to look at her. One day, when I was scouring the parking lot for motorized carts, I saw the strangest thing: the enormous grocery girl had apparently finished her shift for there she was, all 300+ pounds of her, wobbling across the parking lot on a *bike!* My fellow greeter Jim later confirmed that Big Girl and her girlfriend – who also worked at Maytag's – both rode their bikes to work every day, rain or shine. I couldn't help but wonder how, if she was exercising regularly, Big Girl remained so grossly overweight. *More power to her!* I thought. It was certainly more than I did on a daily basis!

There was Rita, who, at 77, was the oldest person working full time hours at Maytag's. Rita was a piece of work unto herself: refusing to follow the directives of various managers, all of whom despaired because she insisted on resting her hind end on the lip of a trash can rather than standing upright on her own two feet as they wished her to do, Rita would regale whoever would listen with stories about everything from the antics of her pets to her latest colonoscopy. I only learned about that when, while she was off work after the procedure, a number of complete strangers walked in the door and asked me whether I knew the results of the test. I was appalled to find out that the old woman had been over-sharing the antics of her *bowels* as well as her cats!

There was Don Lungstrum, who was not only a hell of a nice guy, but also a terrific manager who inspired me to be a better greeter with his calm, measured leadership, and so gets a mention here for being the best manager I've ever worked with.

And there was Nancy, the world's worst greeter. Nancy's personality was so sharp and frigid that frost grew on her extremities in the middle of summer. Absolutely no one liked her. She was bossy, supercilious, and she ratted on everyone who wasn't doing their job correctly, which was, namely, everyone she worked with. Nancy was the anti-greeter, and I was completely mystified as to how any of the hiring managers could have thought she possessed the capacity to make people feel welcome. She actually would've made a great Gestapo officer, should Maytag's have required one, but the need never arose.

The best part of every shift I worked was the fact that Duddy came in to share my breaks with me. I only worked a few hours at a time, but evidently, Dud felt that fifteen minutes with me was worth the drive. He would tell me how his golf game went that day, and I would regale him with tales of horror about the mother who dressed her seven-year old daughter in shoes with high heels, or the lazy people who were clearly perfectly healthy but insisted on using one of the motorized carts anyway, leaving some poor decrepit old geezer having to wait until another one became available. Because Maytag's was a family-owned company, no manager ever said a word about the man who joined me at the café table for those breaks. Indeed, they often gave us smiles of approval.

In spite of all the weirdoes, or perhaps because of them, I rather liked my greeter job. It was a ridiculously easy gig, but also a surprisingly important one: we greeters were the face of Maytag's, and we had the power to make the customers' shopping trips great ones, or, God forbid, really bad ones. And while the rude folks – and they were legion – always got my goat, it was forcing myself to be cheerful for hours at a stretch that really exhausted me. Being nice simply wasn't something I readily embraced; my usual mode with humans was politely taciturn. Nevertheless, I marveled at the idea that I was being paid better than minimum wage to do nothing more than smile and talk to people. If I had to work a job, greeting was the way to go.

Having acquired a job and a live-in boyfriend/fiancée, my life began to take on a sheen of normalcy. I'm sure my therapist was pleased, and thinking that she might just be able to start planning her retirement after all. But while things looked great on paper, the view from inside my head was not so rosy: tucked away in there was still a lifetime's-worth of trauma from having been molested. Even after decades of therapy, there still remained PTSD-related nightmares, poor self-esteem, anger issues, and difficulty getting along with my fellow humans. Time would tell whether Duddy's presence in my life would smooth out some of those rough edges.

What's in a Name?

Back when my beloved Winkie the cat was still alive, I was involved with a man that Winkie didn't like. I should've taken note of that fact, but I didn't. Consequently, I wasted three years on a man that my cat – who turned out to be a better judge of character than I was – knew immediately was not worthy of me. I vowed not to make that same mistake twice.

I was pleased to learn that Duddy had owned dogs *and* cats over the years. It was a good sign, even if my four felines didn't warm up to him right away: nervous as always, they spent the first month or two of our relationship hiding under my bed. I understood – they never readily embraced anyone new in my life, and so didn't press the matter. They would come out and investigate in their own time, and there was no point in trying to rush them.

It was three-legged Gracie Ellen who first extended the paw of friendship. Gracie always was a bit more outgoing than the others, often befriending strangers on the very first meeting. She would bounce her way into the family room, running over to rub up against Dud's leg as he sat on the couch. As he petted her, Gracie would slobber happily and make a succession of satisfied squawking noises.

It didn't take Junebug long to notice that Gracie was getting all the attention. Greedy Junebug liked being at the center of things and would usually hiss at whoever was receiving the fussing, telling them to clear off so that she could enjoy the spotlight. Unfortunately, this made Junebug a bit of a bully, which Duddy found off-putting. "Quit being mean," he'd tell her indignantly. "Gracie gets to have attention, too!" Nonplussed, Junebug would sit staring at him, unsure about his tone, but very definite in her desire to be noticed. It took the boys a bit longer to warm to Dud. For a while, I felt certain that it wouldn't happen at all because of the mocking tone of voice he always used when addressing them.

As I'm sure is the case with every other pet owner on the planet, I have multiple nicknames for each of my cats. Junebug is also My Little Mitten, Honey Bee, and Junebug Gem. Spanky is also Niblet, and Noodle, and Buddy is Wild Man, and Buddy Nip. I don't claim that any of the nicknames make sense, they just *are*, as they are with you and your pets. But Dud apparently found the inclusion of nicknames a comical oddity, and, before I could stop him, he'd begun to create his own for them. I stood shaking my head as he crooned over Spanky – shy Spanky of the poor self-esteem – "Aw, there's my little *cannelloni*! My little bi-colored corn niblet! My *rigatoni spaghetti noodle!*" And then, because I'd turned Dud on to *Downtown Abbey,* "Lord Nibbleton of the Manchester Noodleson's."

"He knows you're making fun of him!" I objected.

"He loves it," Dud replied with a large measure of satisfaction, and indeed, much to my chagrin, there was Spanky, purring happily as Dud ran his hands over him.

Clearly, Spanky relished the extra attention but he wasn't the only one; Buddy was the next to be conquered by Dud's silly ways, even if the same mocking croon did focus on him. "Hi, *Buddy-man!* Hi, *Lord Nipperton!* My *Buddy Ebsen, Jed Clampett cat!*"

"*What?!*" I squawked. "Stop calling him Jed Clampett!" But even I had to laugh, for there was half-feral Buddy, lying on the bed purring as Dud leaned over him, petting his sleek white body. "I can't believe they're falling for this," I said in disgust, "They clearly have no shame whatsoever!"

After Buddy, came Junebug. My Little Mitten became My Little *Minnow*, which, because of her excessive weight, morphed into S. S. Minnow, and then it was only a matter of time before he started singing the *Gilligan's Island* theme song to her. And while I was glad that Dud had passed muster with all the cats, I couldn't believe that they were lapping it all up with such undisguised pleasure! Where was the famous feline reserve?!

As if the new nicknames weren't enough, the boys somehow fell into a Pavlovian routine that continues to this day: Duddy will pat the upholstered rocking chair that Spanky claimed as his own, call, "Where's my Spanky-man?" and Spanky will run from wherever he is, jump up on the chair like the obsequious little butt-kisser he's becoming, and purr happily as Dud pets him. It's an embarrassing display for a specie that has for centuries prided itself on its detachment from its human companions. Buddy's no different: all Dud has to do is go into the bedroom, call for his "Buddy-man!" and wait. Eventually, Buddy will come running and hop up on the bed to be petted. They're a disgrace to cats everywhere!

It must be noted that this is the first time in the history of my four cats that they all like the man I'm involved with. While *I* knew that Dud was the right man for me, I didn't know when or if the cats would figure it out. And if they had decided to dislike him, things might have gone somewhat differently: I might not have invited him to move in with me, for a start.

Dud discovered early on that his place in the household pecking order was *not* at the top of the totem pole. Aghast, he had a few choice words for me the day I asked him to vacate the kitchen so that the cats could eat in peace. "They're fine," he insisted.

"No, they're not. They're afraid to eat with you lurching around the room like that!"

"I'm not *lurching!* And anyway, they're just *cats!*"

"Wrong thing to say to the Critter Lady, dude! Go to jail! Go directly to jail! Do not pass go, do not collect $200!" Dud stared at me incredulously then.

"So the cats are more important than I am?" he asked.

"You have opposable thumbs," I replied, "They don't."

"That's your argument? That they're more important than me because they don't have opposable thumbs?"

"Yep. That's what I'm going with!" He left the room, then, but that would not be the end of the discussion.

"I can't believe that your cats are more important to you than I am!" he said later that day.

"I don't love you *less,* honey, I just love you *differently!*" I said it tongue-in-cheek, but Dud wasn't laughing. "Dud, I'm the *Critter Lady!* I'm always going to *be* the Critter Lady! It's what I do. It's *who I am!*" In time, he would come to understand that, as far as humans go, he was at the top of my list, and that would have to be enough for, as he learned from experience, animals – and not necessarily he – would be, in bad times, my first line of defense. He would come to understand that, and he would come to respect it. The Critter Lady may be crazy, but she also knows how to, in the parlance of the psychological experts, "self-soothe." And self-soothing always, without question, involved critters, even if they *were* called by ridiculous nicknames!

WHAT MONEY BUYS

It goes without saying that for Duddy, getting to know – and learning to live with – a Critter Lady has been an eye-opening experience. He's not accustomed to someone putting the needs of the animals first, and being shooed out of his own kitchen really doesn't sit well with him. The duck who spent several days living in our bathroom gave him pause for thought as well: the smell of duck poop alone was enough to make him wonder about that whole happily-ever-after thing.

To give credit where credit is due, though, I'll say this: Duddy has been a surprisingly good sport about most of my critter peculiarities. At one point, he actually managed to get antibiotic pills down the throat of the aforementioned duck, which impressed the hell out of me. And, he's made friends with half-feral Buddy, a cat who sees little need for relationships of any kind. I have to figure, if Buddy likes him, Dud must be doing something right!

Dud also seems to have embraced volunteering with me at The Harmony Barn. While he's not a big fan of poop scooping, he attends to water bucket cleaning briskly and efficiently. After the buckets are cleaned and refilled (with the help of barn kids Allen and Lydia), he makes the rounds and visits the critters he likes most. At the top of the list is new resident donkey Handsome Harry. Handsome Harry came to the barn via the same place that Cricket did before him – from Kenny the Tiger Guy, who couldn't bring himself to slaughter another perfectly healthy donkey. It seemed almost providential when Kenny called, just weeks after Cricket's death, to say that he had another donkey in need of a home. Wendy immediately agreed to take him.

As he's done with every other volunteer, Harry has charmed Dud by resting his huge head on Dud's shoulder. And while Duddy appears to dismiss my belief that if you talk to animals, they will talk back, I'm fairly certain that he and Harry have had some meaningful conversations when I wasn't there to overhear!

While Dud knew little about horses before we got together, he was intrigued by the concept of leasing a horse, once he knew that such a thing was possible. For those of you who don't know, horses are *very* expensive animals to own. In the first place, there's the monthly cost of boarding, which, in this area, runs about $350 a month. I could buy a decent car for that price! In addition to boarding, there are the fees for the farrier to trim the hooves every six weeks, worming, and dental care. The price can quickly and easily go through the roof. For folks who can't afford all that, leasing can be an option.

Leasing is basically renting a horse. You pay a monthly fee and you get to ride as often as you wish without all the expenses of ownership. I'd never leased a horse before because I couldn't afford it, and I certainly never felt qualified enough: while there's an instructor present during lessons, you ride the leased horse on your own time, when there's generally no one around. It never occurred to me that I might know enough to be able to ride on my own – didn't occur, that is, until I mentioned it to Duddy. He'd been casting about for a suitable gift for my birthday when the subject came up. Knowing how much I loved The Harmony Barn and its horses, he decided that my birthday gift would be his leasing Bit for me!

Through the lessons I had taken on Bit, we were slowly forging a relationship. But leasing him, and figuring out how to fill my time with him, was another matter entirely. You might think that I would just go out to the barn, saddle him up, and hop on every time, but that was not the case. I suppose I *could've* done that, but I wanted more than just to ride around in circles in the arena; that can get boring pretty quickly. So I set myself the task of trying to make him a trail rider.

Since Ruckus died, we'd lost the one bomb-proof horse that could manage a trail ride calmly and smoothly. I knew that Wendy wasn't going to go out and find another trail horse – her mission is rescuing abused horses, and the space available at the barn for that it limited. The obvious solution seemed to be to teach a horse who was already in residence. Since no one had any objection to my idea, I took lead rope in hand and set about showing Bit what the world looked like on the other side of the fence.

There's a u-shaped track that parallels the pasture fence. Ron and Wendy use it to drive the poop-filled tractor out to the back of the property. Bit and I would walk that u-shaped track, stopping often so he could snack on the grass that grows in abundance out there. I made sure, in spite of the numerous times he spooked at something, that every excursion ended positively, with lots of snacks and lots of praise.

Day after day, week after week, we walked that track. When he startled at the corn stalks rustling in the wind on the neighboring property, I pulled a few ears and let him eat them. When he nervously eyed the old wooden wagon filled with junk and sitting forgotten next to the track, I walked him up to it, rapped my knuckles on it, and encouraged him to sniff out its harmlessness. Every scary issue was addressed quickly and confidently to ensure that he didn't harbor any lingering fear of it. And while it sounds like I knew exactly what I was doing in all this, I can assure you that I did not. I made it all up as I went along.

It was precisely because I had no idea what I was doing that I began to wonder whether I was actually making any progress. Perhaps the lack of any specific goals kept me from seeing the small changes as they occurred, but occur they did, and as we repeated this adventure time after time, I began to pick up on them. The most noteworthy change was that Bit spooked less often. All those times I had calmly assured him that everything was o.k. were finally paying off. While that was encouraging, I still wasn't sure whether we were making real, lasting progress until the day I walked out into the mud lot to collect him for yet another walk.

To avoid predictability, I tried to mix up our routine. Some days, I would put a saddle on him before we took our walks so that he would get used to wearing a saddle outside the fence. Other days, I brought Duddy along so that Bit would get used to the presence of distractions. We would walk in different directions on different days, and never stopped to graze at the same place twice. The whole point was to get him accustomed to the idea that strange new things weren't going to harm him and could, in fact, be rather pleasant.

I always groomed Bit, before our walks, and picked his hooves because I saw those things as part of my relationship-building efforts. Due to his EPM balance issues, picking his back hooves could be a real challenge. During lessons, I would have Connie stand in front of Bit to help maintain his focus while I tried to keep from getting kicked. Bit wasn't actually *trying* to kick me, though, he was flailing his back leg because he felt off-balance. Because I would be picking his hooves alone when I leased him, Connie insisted that I learn how to do it all by myself before leasing began. This I ultimately did, and being able to hang on to that flying leg apparently reassured Bit that I could be counted on to handle whatever needed handling. Indeed, I realized that I had succeeded in reassuring Bit that day I went out to collect him for yet another walk.

It was my habit to walk out into the mud lot and call, "Where's Big Boy Bit?" Lately, I had begun to notice that he would drop what he was doing, when he heard my voice, and walk over to me. This particular day, though, he was clearly feeling downright enthusiastic because, much to my considerable surprise, he came trotting around the corner of the barn! In my time on earth, I've had dogs run to greet me, ducks at the pond run to greet me, and even the occasional cat, but never a horse! I was floored! In my search for an indication that my efforts with him were working, Bit's trotting across the mud lot was the proof I needed. We were, indeed, developing a relationship, and Bit's enthusiasm cheered me no end.

I made a point, then, of telling Duddy what a great gift his leasing of Bit was for me. While I certainly enjoyed riding Bit on those occasions when I did, the experience was about so much more than that: my confidence in myself and my horse knowledge was growing by leaps and bounds. In addition, the quiet time spent with Bit did wonders to calm the ever-present chaos in my head – the fallout from having been molested all those years ago. Those chaos-free hours were better medicine than anything the pharmaceutical companies could dream up, and I relished the time I was able to spend alone, quietly, with my best pal, Bit.

I've received some wonderful gifts in my life, but the gift of time with Bit was by far the greatest. We've all heard it said that money can't buy happiness. While I have sneaking suspicions about that – those rich people sure *seem* happy, don't they?! – it's been my experience that money buys *opportunities,* and it is those opportunities that can bring you happiness. Such was the case with Duddy's generous gift. At the time, I had no idea that leasing Bit would be so fulfilling on so many levels, and I marvel, now, at how a modest sum of money brought so much peace and joy to my life. For the first time in my life, thanks to Bit, and to Duddy, I felt truly blessed.

THE GANG

(Part Two)

Given that the *Whoville Journal* regularly published my letters beseeching residents not to put live ducklings in their children's Easter baskets, it was inevitable that the number of domestic ducks living at McKinnon's Pond would naturally decrease over time. Between my entreaties, my Planned Duckhood population control efforts, and the fact that a considerable number of predators made the area their home, the headcount of surviving ducks was now less than ten. Indeed, it had been so long since we'd had a full complement that I could barely remember all the names.

There were Sid, Sol, and Missy Miss, the three who started it all over ten years ago. They were long gone, of course. Of the three ducklings that Missy Miss raised to adulthood – Pretty Boy (my all-time favorite), Pretty Lady, and Big Boy – only Big Boy remained, and he was now so old that after his most recent molt, some of the once-iridescent green feathers on his head grew back in gray. "You're an old man, now, Big Boy!" I would tell him during feeds. He hadn't slowed down much; he still managed to shoulder his way to the front of the pack at feeding time, just as Pretty Boy had done.

There were Frick and Frack, two gregarious Pekins who charmed me incessantly with their friendly natures. I couldn't even remember how long they'd been gone. There were Ducky, and Puddleduck, Handsome, Junior, and Peepers – all five of whom became lame and ended up being adopted by Pat and Pete Mitchell. Of the five, only Ducky and Handsome are still alive now. I continue to visit them two or three times a year, tossing bread and chattering away in the tone of voice they had become accustomed to at the pond. Much to Pat Mitchell's surprise, they still remember me after all these years!

Girlfriend Duck, who had been Pretty Boy's mate, developed an infection. She spent a few days in the bathroom while Dud and I treated her with antibiotics. She ended up going to the same farm that adopted the six nameless Pekins that Officer Dave and I had rescued.

And there were Pretty Girl, mate of Handsome, and Mama Duck, mother of Little Nipper, the injured duckling who spent a week in my bathroom. Both had been taken by predators several years back. And there were Ethel and Boyfriend Duck. You'll read more about them later.

I have fond memories of all the ducks in my care, and the special relationships I enjoyed with each of them. Every duck had a different temperament, and a different personality. Some, like Frick, Frack, and Pretty Boy, were so outgoing and fearless that they would eat right out of my hand, standing so close in the process that we frequently touched. Owing to multiple health issues over the years, Pretty Boy got used to being handled. It never stopped him from biting me, but he pulled his punches and never bit hard enough to do anything more than express his irritation.

Other ducks remained shy through the years, never developing much in the way of trust. Missy Miss always shied away when I tried to pet her, as did many of the others. It seemed as though the ones who had health issues – and had, therefore, been handled – became more trusting than those who hadn't, as though they knew intrinsically that I was trying to help them. They all came to know me, though, as the person with the bag of corn, who could be counted on to feed them when no other means of sustenance could be found.

There were many times, over the years, that pedestrians and car drivers alike would slow down – or stop completely in the middle of the road! – to watch the spectacle on the beach: there I was, the Pied Piper of Whoville, sitting on the ground, surrounded by twenty ducks or more (most of whom were wild Mallards), every one of us talking – or quacking – as though we were the best of friends. And in a way, we were: no one ever knew those ducks as intimately as I did. No one knew their individual personalities like I did. The only one who came close was Pat Mitchell, but even she had curtailed her daily feeds as the years went by.

The few remaining ducks still required my attention: Freckle Duck got a fish hook stuck in her throat that Dr. Sue thankfully managed to extricate. Little Nipper had grown into an adult with no trace of a limp whatsoever, and eventually overcame his wariness with me to the point that he, too, would now stick his head in the bag of corn. His sister, Little Peeps, was too shy to wade into the mass of greedy ducks, which always made me worry that she wasn't getting enough to eat. And Big Boy was such an old man that something bad was *bound* to happen to him sooner or later. In addition, there were three other hybrids – offspring of a domestic girl (I no longer remember who) and a wild mallard – who I'd never gotten around to naming. Those seven ducks were all that remained of what had once been a much bigger cast of characters.

I still made the ten-minute drive to the pond three times a week. I still wrote my annual Easter letter to the *Whoville Journal*. I still enjoyed a small but generous following of duck fans who regularly donated cracked corn to my Luckey Duck Fund – indeed, I hadn't actually had to buy a bag of corn in several years; the duck fans kept them well-supplied. And I still advocated for those who were ill or injured.

But my time as the McKinnon's Pond Duck Lady was winding down, and I began to conceive of a time when there would – hopefully – be no more abandoned flightless ducks to look after. I had been caring for the ducks for a very long time: thirteen years, and so many ducks that I couldn't begin to count them all. But spreading my emotions so thinly, thinly enough that *all* the creatures in my care – ducks, cats, horses, etc. – enjoyed an equal share of my time and energy, was exhausting work, and I was feeling a little tired. Having acquired not one but *two* duck-feeding volunteers, the time seemed right to slow things down a bit; to sleep in once in a while, and turn some of my attention to other things.

Among my official Disability diagnoses is this one: Borderline Personality Disorder. Loosely translated, it means "doesn't play well with others." Humans are a thorny bunch, and for as long as I can remember, I've had trouble getting along with them. Over the years, countless friends have fallen by the wayside, unfortunate debris in the wreckage that is my life. Every now and then, though, someone special comes along.

A NON-CRITTER CHAPTER

Duddy's previous existence had been so chaotic for so long that he didn't bring much of anything with him when he moved into the Critter Shack. Even the few items of clothing he owned were outdated and ill-fitting, requiring – happily – several trips to my favorite place, the second-hand clothing store. By the time we'd finished, he had a wardrobe to rival any other sharp-dressed man in the neighborhood, given that my favorite store sold brand name items at incredible discounts. Dud *did* bring one thing of value with him, though, and that was his friends. First and foremost among them were Dave and Lynnette.

I've never had much trouble making friends; *keeping* them was a different matter. More often than not, I would at some point shoot off my mouth about a sensitive subject, thoroughly alienating my friend in the process. Keeping my opinions to myself was never my strong suit, and given a choice between speaking an ugly truth or saying nothing, I invariably chose to say my piece, consequences be damned. I can't say that I missed too many of the casualties after they were gone – they were often as dysfunctional as I was – but the body count *was* a little alarming. After a while, it seemed easier to just avoid friendships altogether. Unfortunately, Dud was an extrovert, requiring me to make the occasional compromise to my usual isolationist tendencies. In this regard, though it was always an emotional struggle for me, I was willing to get together with Dud's friends for the occasional dinner out.

I first met Lynnette when Dud brought me along to her house. She and Dave were selling the house and moving themselves and their two cats onto a boat in Florida. Since space on the boat would be at a premium, Lynnette had offered us some of her cat-related paraphernalia, and Dud wanted me to come along and take my pick from the various items. As I considered the offerings, I noted that Lynnette was an instantly-likeable woman, with a keen intelligence and a quick wit. She owned her own marketing firm, and she was about to embark on the sort of dream life that I had never had the courage to attempt myself: their dream was life on a boat, mine had been life in London. I had allowed so many things to hold me back that I was doubly impressed that she and Dave were actually in the process of making their dream happen. How often do you meet people like that?

While I can't say that I know Dave well, I can report that he's an affable fellow, the mellow yin to Lynnette's exuberant yang. Watching the two of them together, it's clear that while Lynnette is the kite, flying happily around the stratosphere, Dave is firmly on the ground, holding the string. It seems to be a mutually agreeable arrangement.

We went to the theatre with them once. After the performance, not wanting the night to end just yet, the four of us decided to have coffee and dessert at a nearby restaurant. We sat around the table feeling marginally uneasy about the fact that we were the only people in the entire establishment.

Indeed, the owner himself decided to wait on us, rather than keeping staff on hand who would otherwise have gone home. He assured us that he was happy to have us there, though, and indicated that we should take all the time we wanted to enjoy ourselves.

As I sat across the table from Dave, I noted that his shirt was of a style that I was familiar with. When I said as much, Lynnette piped up, "It's like –"

"Yes," I replied, interrupting her in mid-sentence.

"From the –"

"Yes," I said, again in mid-sentence. She immediately turned to Dave and said accusingly, "It took *years* before you understood me that well!" By the look on his face, he was clearly mystified. "What are you two *talking* about?!"

"Your shirt," I responded. "Charlie Sheen wore shirts just like that in *Two and a Half Men*." Lynnette and I grinned at each other then, and I've no doubt that we were thinking along the same lines: *there's a friendship in the making here!* Unfortunately, she and her husband were in the process of packing what little they planned to use aboard their new 50-foot boat, and would, in a month's time, be moving permanently out of state. My only consolation was that Lynnette would be coming back to Whoville every month on company business.

When I turned the matter over in my head, though, I realized that a part-time friendship might be better suited to someone of my reserved nature. Full-time friendships hadn't worked out well for me; maybe spending less time together was the key to success. I liked Lynnette immensely, and it was the first friendship I'd kindled with a reasonably-sane person. Perhaps if I attempted a reasonable degree of sanity myself, the relationship stood a better chance of working out. Naturally, only time would tell.

GRACIE ELLEN TRIPOD

As I mentioned in *Crazy Critter Lady,* I adopted three-legged Gracie mainly by default: I had found her dragging her useless fourth leg around my therapist's parking lot one day. In addition to her injury, she turned out to be pregnant as well – two things, as bad luck would have it, that the local humane society didn't care to invest time or money in. When I tried to drop her off there, the girl on duty politely told me that a cat in Gracie's condition didn't stand much chance of living the rest of the day, let alone the rest of her life. I took Gracie to the chicken coop, and while I made feeble attempts to find her a new home, she made herself comfortable in mine. She's been with me ever since.

Gracie spent several years being fairly reserved. She slept a lot, ate some, and avoided the other cats much of the time. In retrospect, she avoided Muffin far more than any of the others. That may have been because Muff was so angry by the addition of Gracie that she refused to extend the paw of friendship. Long after the other cats had accepted Gracie into the fold, Muffin still growled angrily when Gracie got too close. Once Muff died, though, and the social hierarchy changed, Gracie became surprisingly friendly, snuggling with me on the bed at night, and joining me on the couch for some t.v. in the evenings. She purred happily whenever I petted her, and slobbered buckets of drool in the process: Gracie had a good life going, and she knew it.

She hated Spanky with a passion. Playful Spanky, in need of a new mom after Muffin passed, clearly hoped that Gracie would pick up where Muff left off. But Gracie was having none of it, and her outraged screeches, whenever Spanky pounced on her, reverberated throughout the house. *"Spanky!"* I'd thunder, "why is it always you?!" When I'd go to break up the altercation, Spanky would always slink guiltily away. This sort of thing went on all the time; he never seemed to get the hint.

"She *doesn't like you,* Spanky!" I'd tell him. He refused to believe such a thing was possible.

"Gracie? Are you o.k.?" From the depths of the closet, I'd hear her growl in response: *I hate him, Kelly!*

"I know you do, Gracie." What more could I say? All she wanted was to be left in peace and Spanky foiled her at least once every single day. She took to hiding behind the refrigerator, which caused me no end of worry, those times I couldn't find her and thought she might've somehow escaped the house. Her other hiding place was behind the washer. It got to the point where, if Spanky so much as walked into a room that she was in, she'd start growling, which made for very close quarters indeed.

"Gracie, Spanky lives here, too. He's not bothering you, so stop growling!"

Yes, he is, Kelly! He bothers me! Meaning, of course, that the mere sight of him annoyed her.

"Get over it, Gracie! We all have to get along!"

While Gracie had settled happily into her life with me – and learned to live with being, like the others, spoiled rotten – there was one area in which she retained a bit of her street-wise ways: food. Even though there was almost always a bowl of kibble on the kitchen floor, Gracie always acted as though she didn't know when – or if – her next meal was coming. I learned the hard way to hide things inside the microwave because if I left them on the counter, she would invariably jump up and eat them. Whether it was a cut of meat thawing for dinner, or a flavored muffin from the bakery, she would eat almost anything.

"Gracie, why did you eat my muffin? I leave kibble out for you *every single day!*"

I'm not sure, Kelly! She didn't mean that she didn't have an answer; what she meant was, she wasn't sure that I would, indeed, leave her kibble every single day. Even after seven years of living the life of Riley, Gracie still didn't entirely trust her position or my good intentions. It made me a little sad.

When Duddy came onto the scene and into the house, Gracie viewed him as another prospective Gracie-petter and she'd jump enthusiastically on the bed every night, hoping for some of his attention. If she didn't pass the night snuggling by my side, she could invariably be found snuggling by his. She was clearly thrilled to have an extra human around, and availed herself of him many times every day. As far as she was concerned, Dud was her buddy, and she manufactured copious amounts of slobber just for him.

When I first brought Muffin home from the shelter, she was a reserved three-year old adult cat. At seven, while she would never be as refined and ladylike as Muffin had been, Gracie had settled calmly into feline middle-age. Like Muff, she enjoyed a good snuggle – something I'd sorely missed since Muffin passed – and, like Muff, Gracie behaved and minded her manners. Gracie would never be anything like Muffin, of course, but her gentleness reminded me of my time with Muffin and soothed something that had been lonely in me since she died.

I particularly enjoyed our evenings on the couch. At some point, Gracie would join us in the family room, insisting on lying next to me on the couch. If I petted her for too long, or if she wanted to play a little, she would bite me very carefully, taking special care not to break my skin. After a minute or two of this, she would curl up and nap while Dud and I watched t.v. Within minutes of our going to bed, she would join us, usually staking out a place near my pillow. She was a carefree cat who asked for little, but gave so much quiet pleasure in return. Even Dud couldn't help but be charmed by her engaging personality.

LEARNING THE HARD WAY

As winter approached, and the opportunity to ride Bit lessened, I decided to put the cold months to good use teaching him some ground manners. This was because when anyone tried to climb into the saddle, Bit would foil them by refusing to stand still. He'd walk this way and that, backward and forward, in his attempts to keep them from getting on his back. This was not only annoying, but dangerous, too, and while I'd never actually taught a horse anything before, I figured that ground manners were worth a shot.

I wish I could say that I'd been 100% successful with that endeavor, but Bit has a strong personality, so we tended to butt heads a lot. Any number of times, during our sessions, he would turn his head toward me, take the loose end of the lead rope in his mouth, and repeatedly flail his head about. It was his way of saying, *Enough already! I know how to do this!* To which I always replied, "You might know how to do it, but you don't know how to do it *well!*" Clearly Bit and I disagreed on how much for training he needed to have.

I tried working with Bit on a regular basis, but sometimes, it was just too cold for my delicate constitution. Even inside the arena, the penetrating cold would numb my fingers to the point where I couldn't properly fasten the tack. So there were times when we went a number of days between sessions, and Bit always liked to pretend that he'd forgotten what I taught him.

Repeatedly, I would walk him up to the mounting block, bring him to a halt, and try to climb into the saddle – only to watch him back away at the last minute. Around in a circle we'd walk, and I'd line him up with the mounting block again – and again, each time attempting a safe mount, and each time watching him back away from the block. Ugh! Fortunately, toward the end of our sessions, he'd do things correctly a couple of times and I'd reward him with an apple slice. Suffice to say the learning came at a glacial pace.

It didn't help that ground work was all we could do. If it wasn't too cold to attempt a walk outside, then the ground was too muddy to walk in, all of which confounded my efforts to work with him outside the fence. We had spent a lot of quality time together in the fall, walking the track outside the fence. Our walks consisted mainly of Bit eating grass, Bit startling at something imaginary, Bit prancing nervous circles around me, and me standing calmly by, reassuring him in a soothing tone of voice that all was well. By the time winter hit and it was too cold to continue our walks, Bit had calmed down considerably, and I had begun to feel somewhat optimistic about using him as a trail horse. I should've known that my optimism was misplaced!

When the first hint of spring weather arrived, and the muddy track finally dried up, I decided to break up the winter monotony and take Bit out for a walk around the track. Unfortunately, he spooked at so many things that it was like taking him out for the very first time all over again. Even so, he did pretty good for a 'fraidy horse, and we managed to make it all the way back to the end of the property. I made sure to let him stop and graze on what little grass there was at every opportunity because grazing always seemed to calm him down. It was while he grazed that I decided to walk him even further still.

The trail-riding track runs along the back edge of several properties. On one side is a long row of evergreen shrubs that border the properties, and Bit did very well walking the length of it. After giving him a chance to look and see and smell, I turned and headed back toward the barn. It was as we rounded the back corner of Wendy's property that the thing I always feared finally happened: Bit spooked and shot off at a gallop. All the previous times that Bit startled, he never ran any farther than the lead rope would stretch. But this time was different, and in the split second after he took off, several thoughts crossed my mind in quick succession:

If I don't let go of the lead rope, I could lose some fingers!
I'll never be able to catch him!
He's not going to come if I call!
God, I hope he doesn't run out into the road!

I had let go of the lead rope and watched as it trailed alongside him. If I'd hung onto it it could've tightened around my hand and literally ripped my fingers off. Helplessly, I watched Bit tear across the field, drawing a momentary blank as to what to do next. Then it occurred to me: *Call Ron!*

The only reason I had my phone with me was because Wendy had suggested it when I started leasing Bit. The idea made sense: co-owner Ron was almost always somewhere on the property, and he was universally recognized as the alpha horse. Unfortunately, my phone decided not to cooperate when I tried dialing Ron's number. I paused in despair, wondering what the hell to do now, and thinking about how, if something bad happened to Bit, it would be my fault. In the midst of all that thought, I almost didn't notice that Bit had changed his trajectory and was now running directly toward the mud lot where his herd was. When he reached the mud lot fence, he stopped running. That was unexpected!

Fortunately for all concerned, I had the presence of mind to remember the advice I'd gotten from both Wendy and Connie: that in order to teach Bit to be calm, *I* must exude calm. Fighting my desire to run up the track to retrieve Bit, I walked instead. While every inch of my being wanted to race to where he was so that I could regain control, I knew that doing so would only confirm to him that there was, indeed, something to be afraid of, and that he would probably take off running again.

So I strolled at our usual walking pace, forcing myself to remain cool and collected. And, because prey animals have very good hearing, I began to talk to him, too, softly giving my usual running commentary about what a nice day it was to be a horse, and what a big, goofy meatball he was. To my everlasting surprise, it worked! When I was half-way up the track, Bit turned his head, saw me coming, and trotted a few paces in my direction. Then he stopped and stood stock still, facing me and waiting for me to come and get him. It was clear in that moment that he was thinking, *Kelly's here! Everything's o.k. now!*

It was one of those incredible moments that I don't get to see very often, the kind of moment in which Bit shows me that we have, indeed, been building a relationship, and that I've earned his trust. In all those teaching sessions where he'd get impatient and grab the lead rope, it sure didn't *seem* as though we were accomplishing much. And yet, there he was, trotting eagerly toward me and then stopping to wait for me to catch up. Once I did, I took possession of the lead rope that was still attached to his halter, gave him a couple of snacks, and heaped praise on him for being such a smart boy. Then, because I wanted things to end on a normal note rather than a panicked one, I let him graze a little, and then led him into the barn to be groomed.

In my experiences with Bit, whether we're working on a new skill or just hanging out, I'm learning that John Lennon's words, *Life is what happens to you while you're busy making other plans,* are true. While I'm focused on the tasks at hand, and assuming that Bit is, too, something intangible is happening: we're getting to know each other in subtle ways, ways that apparently reassure him that I'm safe, and that I'll keep him safe. That I'm reliable and that he can rely on me. Such important things, and such a shame that we never notice them unless we're tasked with a situation that brings them to the fore. I suspect that the same is true of human relationships, too.

So while the thing I feared most did, indeed, happen, I came away from it feeling very reassured about my knowledge as a horsewoman (disaster did not befall us after all), and about my relationship with Bit (who, contrary to his usual behavior, has actually learned a few things). There's nothing better than realizing that you know a little more than you thought you did!

Oh – the thing that sent Bit galloping across the field? A white plastic grocery bag wafting on the breeze. Who knew something so inconsequential could be so terrifying?

Despite all the evidence around him, Duddy appeared to have no idea how firmly entrenched I was in my involvement with animals. He seemed to think of it as my amusing little hobby, rather than the lifetime commitment that it actually was. Initially, he would push back against the critter tsunami, hoping to keep it at bay. After a time, he realized that because caring for animals was <u>my</u> destiny, it would become his, as well.

WE'VE GOT DUCKS!

I suppose it was inevitable that I would one day bring some domestic ducks home from the pond to stay. I don't know why I never did it with Pretty Boy – who would have made a charming addition to my critter menagerie – except that it never seemed particularly do-able. For one reason or another, I just didn't feel prepared for the task: there would need to be a pen, and a water feature of some sort, and a whole lot more security than I felt I had at my disposal. So injured ducks were always returned to McKinnon's Pond once they'd been rehabbed. It wasn't the best solution, but it was the obvious one. And it worked fine right up until Boyfriend Duck developed a noticeable limp.

Boyfriend Duck was the mate of my new favorite duck, Ethel, who had come to the fore after Pretty Boy's death. Always cheerful, and far more trusting than any of the other ducks, Ethel was the bright spot in every day that I saw her. She and Boyfriend spent the majority of their time on the far side of pond, away from the other ducks. They would all come together in the winter and share the open water around the City fountain, but for most of the rest of the year, Ethel and Boyfriend preferred the peace and quiet of the far side, where few people ever went.

I always went looking for them. I'd feed the domestics who milled around in front of the boathouse, then strike off around the side of the pond, calling as I went, "Ethel-Ethel! Where's a pretty girl?" At some point, both ducks would come running toward me, stopping at the last minute before they crashed into my legs or the bag of cracked corn. Because we'd built up quite a relationship over the years, the two of them would actually climb *in* the bag of corn rather than eat what was on the ground. Climbing into the bag meant that they could neither see nor hear what was going on outside, which showed me how much trust they'd invested in the giant human who was chatting away outside the bag. That trust in me was what made our relationship so special, and I was proud to show off this feature of it to whoever came along with me.

It was Duddy who came with me, the day I noticed Boyfriend's limp. "He won't survive the winter on the ice with that limp," I remarked. Dud said nothing. He probably had no idea what I was talking about, let alone where my mind had gone after that initial thought. I didn't say anything more about it, but I was thinking that at some point, there would need to be a rescue, and a decision made about what to do next. I gave it a few days, then mentioned the limp again. This time, I added, "He's going to need a new home, and so will Ethel. I wouldn't dream of splitting them up." I let him chew on that for a few days before I pressed the point further.

"Boyfriend and Ethel are going to need a home. He won't survive on the pond this winter. He'll slip and fall and not be able to get up. Then he'll lie out there and die a horrible death. What do you think about bringing them back here to live?

"*Here?*" Dud queried in disbelief, as though I had just asked if we might bring home a rabid wolverine.

"They wouldn't be any trouble, once we got them situated."

"They'd wreck the lawn!" he exclaimed, as though this was the major consideration.

"How much damage to you really think a couple of ducks can do?" I ventured cautiously, not wanting to inflame the discussion any further.

"Why don't we wait and see if he recovers, and take it from there," came the reply. It was as good an answer as I was going to get so I let it go for a week or two.

"That limp isn't getting any better," I reported, "we're going to need to do something before fall comes. In the fall, they all get jiggy because of hunting season and I won't be able to catch anyone until spring. He'll be dead by then. If we're going to do this, we need to do it soon." A lively debate (read: heated argument) ensued then about whether one's responsibilities extended to include adopting homeless ducks.

"I'm the *Critter Lady,* for God's sake! This sort of thing *is* my responsibility!"

"Why can't we find them a nice home somewhere?" Dud tried to reason, to which I replied that if there *were* good loving homes for ducks, I'd have found them by now, over ten years into my McKinnon's Pond commitment.

"It's us, or he dies. It's just that simple." And while Dud saw the truth in that, and went along with the idea, there was a fair amount of grumbling about it not being *his* responsibility.

"I get no say in this!" he said angrily.

"You *do* get a say, Dud, you just don't get veto power!"

At that point, I gave things a few days to settle down before I brought up the subject of the duck pen he would need to build. It should be up off the ground, I said, with a door that opened up into a ramp that they could walk down. Beyond that, my ideas were fairly vague, but he seemed to grasp the concept, and after turning the matter over in his head – and realizing that there was no getting out from under our impending duck ownership – he announced that he had a plan in mind. The only question left was when he might actually start building.

A week passed. Well into Week Two, I remarked, "If something happens to Boyfriend Duck while you're busy procrastinating, I'll hold it against you forever!"

"No, you won't," he answered as he peered at me over his glasses.

"Oh, yes, I will, and that's a promise from me to you!" He peered again, no doubt trying to gauge the severity of my threat.

"I'll get it done," he said in that tone men use when they're hoping you'll drop the subject.

"*When?*"

"This week," came the vague reply. I let it go at that, knowing full well that we'd be deep into Week 3 before my nagging sufficiently moved him to take action.

In truth, I was doing some procrastinating myself. Adding two more animals to the list of residents at the Critter Shack meant adding more duties to the daily roster. Not to mention more chances for something to go horribly wrong if I didn't cover all my bases. In my on-going struggle with depression, the last thing I needed was more responsibility. Still, every time I wrestled with the matter in my head, I knew that bringing Ethel and Boyfriend home was the right thing to do; there was simply no way he would survive the winter with that limp, and I definitely didn't want his death on my hands.

The swearing began almost immediately after construction did. "Goddammit!" Dud hollered loud enough for neighbor Russell to hear, "I hate this stupid drill!" Hating the drill became such a mantra that I half expected Dud to stop building altogether. To his credit, though, he persevered, putting in a few hours here and there as his schedule allowed. Happily, once Dud started a project, he liked to keep going until he finished – even if it *was* just a pen for some dumb old ducks!

I kept reassuring him that once the ducks were settled in, he would be thoroughly charmed by them, but he remained skeptical. Never having experienced ducks before, it was obvious that he thought they would be more trouble than they were worth. Which made his determination to build a nice duck pen for me all the more endearing.

As if the problematic drill weren't bad enough, though, the mounting price tag for the project really rankled. "Do you know what this has cost so far?" he asked me irritably, *"for a duck pen?!"* I gave him my best sympathetic look and said nothing. Given that I had accompanied him to the big box hardware store, I knew exactly what it was costing, and it was a fair chunk of change we were spending. As construction continued, Dud made several trips back to the store, trading in extra, unneeded items for bits and pieces that he only thought of as work progressed. Clearly, in Dud's mind, it might only be a duck pen, but if he was going to put the time and effort into it, it was going to be a damn nice duck pen!

"What do you think, honey?" he asked, standing back to survey his work. He had done a fine job, and I told him so. Given that I had only provided those few vague ideas – the gauge of the fencing for the floor and door had to be small enough that raccoons couldn't get their hands through, but big enough that a duck's toenail wouldn't be torn off by; the fact that the pen needed to be tall enough for them to stand up straight in – he had created a simple but sturdy home which would keep the ducks safe and secure during the night.

While Duddy was busy building the pen, I spent a considerable amount of time mentally rehearsing how we would capture the ducks. It was important to grab them both at more or less the same time because if we didn't, the remaining duck was sure to keep his or her distance from me for an indeterminate amount of time afterward.

In addition, it was crucial that we grab them sooner rather than later: every single fall, without fail, the ducks become wary of all humans, including me. It's as though they know when hunting season has begun, even though the domestics are never in any danger whatsoever, living, as they do, on a City pond where hunting is prohibited. Evidently, though, word travels in duck circles, making them all but impossible to catch, and there's not a thing I can do to alleviate their concern. Their wariness generally lasts until spring.

My ideal plan involved me grabbing both ducks myself in one fell swoop. The fact that they'd both become accustomed to climbing into the twenty-five pound bag of corn would make them, in my estimation, that much easier to catch. I intended to use their trust to my advantage, so I envisioned a scenario – based on reality – where Ethel would be standing beside me while Boyfriend climbed into the bag. I could easily pick her up and pin her wings against me with my arm while I pushed Boyfriend's butt into the bag, which I would then grab the top of.

Naturally, my plan would probably only work in that perfect world/parallel universe that doesn't actually exist! Which is why I formulated Plan B. Plan B involved me coaching Dud, who would be standing some distance away from the actual feed. The minute I grabbed Ethel, I would give him the signal to chase Boyfriend with a large beach towel, trying to cover Boyfriend with it before he managed to reach the water. It was do-able, but it wasn't a great plan.

The reason it wasn't a great plan had to do with my skepticism about Duddy's ability to catch a duck. You might think it's an easy thing to do, but I'm here to tell you otherwise! Those little guys are a lot faster than you might think, and once they reach the water, they have the home court advantage. In addition, once you've tried something as treacherous as this, they won't trust you again for quite some time. And while *I* knew all of this from personal experience, Dud did *not*. Which was why, when the opportunity presented itself a day earlier than planned, I went for it all by myself and managed to grab both ducks in a perfect execution of Plan A.

I hadn't actually intended to try grabbing them that day, but I knew from previous experience that it was a now-or-never situation that I needed to take advantage of. Once I had them, though, I was at a momentary loss for what to do next: I hadn't bothered getting the critter carrier out of the trunk, and now here I was with one duck squirming under my arm and the other grumbling loudly from inside the bag.

I set the bag down, popped the trunk latch, and managed to fish the carrier out. I got Ethel into it easily enough, but I had my doubts about being able to put Boyfriend in as well without Ethel hopping out. I pulled him out of the bag and held him in my arms while I thought about what to do next. Unlike Ethel, Boyfriend held still, no doubt wondering what the hell was going on. I told him I thought it would be easier if he went back in the bag for the ride to the house.

Boyfriend: *I'm not going back in the bag, Kelly!*

Kelly: "Then you're going to have to share the carrier with Ethel."

Boyfriend: *Fine.*

And without a lick of fuss, into the carrier he went.

When I got back to the house, I put both ducks immediately into the pen, along with bowls of corn, water, and mixed fresh fruit. They were deeply unhappy about the turn of events. I decided to leave them in the pen overnight, and then let them go out into the yard the next day. Again, from experience, I knew that they would need to acclimate in their own good time. Unfortunately, Dud – who at times appears to display all the characteristics of someone with ADD – had other ideas.

"Let's let them out now," he suggested.

"No, I want to leave them in there overnight," I replied.

"Let's let them out now!" he said again, apparently assuming I hadn't heard him the first time.

"No, they need to get acclimated. They're frightened and they need to settle in a bit. I'll let them out tomorrow."

"How about if we let them out now!" he repeated, grinning because he knew he was getting on my nerves.

"How about if you go away and leave them alone?!" I retorted. Which is eventually what he did when he realized that the ducks would not be coming out of the pen that day.

SPANKY

As I mentioned in *Crazy Critter Lady,* Spanky the cat suffers from low self-esteem. I never figured out why, exactly, I just know that he does. And while I've made a concerted effort to assuage some of his insecurity, there remains in him a level of melancholy that no amount of attention could dispel. He can frequently be found mooning around the kitchen, wailing unhappily. "Your life is *not* a misery, Spanky!" I tell him impatiently. That only makes him wail more.

The good news is that he basks in the attention Dud showers him with, purring happily as he runs to his chair like Pavlov's Cat, waiting for Dud to tell him what a good boy he is. It's an embarrassing display for a specie that prides itself on its aloofness, but as long as Spanky is getting something he needs, I'm happy for him. And, it must be said that Dud's affection seems to be just what Spanky needed in the wake of Muffin's death.

Losing his mommy-cat was a huge blow, one that Spanky's never completely gotten over. Muff had tended to his needs since I brought him home as a kitten, and there was now currently no one in the house who was willing to take over the job. While he makes frequent requests of Gracie, she wants nothing to do with him. Junebug doesn't seem to have a nurturing bone in her body, and Buddy just likes to lord it over him and chase him around the house from time to time. After all that, it's no wonder Spanky began to feel like no one (no one on four legs, anyway) loved him. Dud's attention clearly came as a welcome relief.

There are any number of times, throughout a given day, that Dud will return home from an errand and Spanky will immediately run to his chair, knowing that once he gets there, Dud will fawn all over him. If Duddy fails to do so immediately – that is to say, if he decides to talk to me before he attends to Spanky – I instantly reproach him, saying, "You can't turn him into Pavlov's Cat and then *not* reward him when he does what you've taught him!" To which Dud will roll his eyes, knowing that he isn't going to get anywhere with me until he's given Spanky some attention.

And while you'd think that all the extra love would turn him into a spoiled brat, I can assure you that it has not. Spanky continues to have a streak of depression in him no matter how much or how often we tell him that we love him. It's as if there's a part of him that's unreachable, a sad spot in his otherwise optimistic heart that never allows him to be too happy for too long, and no amount of reassurance seems to change that.

The charming thing about Spanky is that he clearly still thinks he's a kitten. Even though he's now, at eleven years old, firmly on the back side of middle-age, Spanky still plays like a kitten, acts like a kitten, and needs attention from the grown-up cats like a kitten. He's forever getting into mischief by trying to engage the other cats in play when all they want to do is nap. He'll pounce on them, rudely waking them from their slumber, and he never seems to understand why that angers them. If he can't rouse one of them, he'll go looking for trouble on top of the dining room table. Many times, I've walked into the kitchen to find that a Tootsie Pop which had been on the table is now lying on the floor. I know full well who's moved it, even if I can't prove it.

He is by far the prettiest orange tabby I've ever seen, and his big green eyes are the most expressive. He'll look at me with such earnestness when I comb him, clearly hoping that the things I'm saying – "You're *such* a pretty 'Panky! You're the best orange tabby in the whole world!" – are true. He'll gaze at Duddy with the same expression, and it's obvious that he thinks Dud is his best friend.

I happened to mention to Dud that I'd taught both Buddy and Spanky to walk on a leash. Intrigued, Dud immediately announced that he wanted to do it, too. So I brought out the harness and leash, hooked Spanky up, then proceeded to follow the two of them around the back yard, snapping numerous pictures. "Just let him go where he wants to go, and quietly follow him," I instructed.

They did quite well together, wandering around in the ivy, and sniffing all the shrubs – there are several neighborhood cats who routinely mark our yard with their scent – and I couldn't resist posting a few of the pictures on Facebook, above the caption, "A man and his cat: it's a beautiful thing!" Dud and Spanky both seem to have enjoyed the outing, which means I can count on Dud to make it a regular feature, which, as it happens, is just the sort of thing that Spanky needs in order to feel special. Happily, Dud doesn't seem to be put off by Spanky's neediness; indeed, he responds to it quite lovingly. I could not have asked for more in a man.

THE BIG DAY

It was barn-owner Wendy who gave me the idea when she asked, "Are you going to ride Bit during your wedding?" The question arose because, after careful thought, Duddy and I decided to hold our wedding in Ron and Wendy's arena. It made sense, given that we continued to volunteer at the barn, as well as lease Bit. But I hadn't thought about using Bit in the ceremony, though, until Wendy asked her question. When I turned the matter over in my mind, I thought, *why not?*

I had spent the winter working on Bit's ground manners. This consisted mainly of teaching him about the mounting block and how it works. And although I spent at least a couple of days every week working on that, I met with very limited success. No matter what I tried, Bit didn't seem to learn much, or grasp what he was meant to do. Finally, in desperation, I scheduled a lesson with Connie, my riding instructor.

In less than five minutes, she figured out what I needed to do in order to get Bit to do what he needed to do. Things suddenly became so clear that I kicked myself inwardly and asked the unanswerable question, *why don't I think of these things first and save myself the agony?*

Once I started doing things the way Connie taught me, it was time to move on to the next step. Step Two involved teaching Bit the routine we were to perform at the wedding. While I hadn't initially planned on including a horse in the wedding, once Wendy and I discussed it, and the idea was in my head, I ran with it and decided that it might be really cool to make Bit part of the ceremony. Given that Duddy would be doing what he does best – playing guitar – it made sense to incorporate one of my favorite things, too.

Having Bit participate in the wedding presented a few challenges. First, how would he behave with fifty people sitting on a set of rental bleachers in his usually-empty arena? How would he react to two guys playing guitar? What if he didn't do what I asked of him at the crucial moment? Wendy and Connie both thought things would go well, but I personally am a worrier: if I can't control the outcome, I get a little nervous!

So we practiced. And practiced. We practiced while Duddy stood in the arena playing guitar. We practiced using the mounting block in the aisle – a thing that normally isn't done for safety reasons. We practiced so much that Bit began to anticipate my commands, forcing me to get creative during training sessions: I frequently changed things up by altering the direction we walked in, or walking past our cue instead of trotting, to throw him off a little. The point was to familiarize him with the routine without allowing him to take over. It must be said, though, that ours wasn't a big routine, or particularly taxing; it was simply that Bit had never been tasked with performing at a wedding before.

On the Big Day, we tried to work out any final kinks that Bit might have. Connie suggested that I longe Bit in order to get some of the piss and vinegar out of him, which Mandy, as my Maid of Honor, willingly did for me. When she finished longeing him, she tacked him up so that I wouldn't get my wedding clothes dirty doing it myself. Once he was saddled, I put a lead rope on him and took him out into the arena. We poked our heads out one of the big arena doors and had a look around, and then I walked him over to the folding chairs where Dud and his accompanist would sit. I rapped the metal chair with my knuckles so that Bit could get a sense of it, and then I strummed the guitar that was propped against it. I let Bit see the people filling the stands, as well. We stood for a couple of minutes taking it all in: I didn't want there to be any surprises for him.

In the minutes before our routine, Bit got fussy. I had planned for this by asking barn co-owner Ron to help me in the aisle. Connie volunteered her services, too, so that I had two horse experts – one of whom was the recognized head of the herd — available to help allay any jitters Bit may have had. I didn't count on Bit getting agitated, though; I had assumed that Ron's presence would take care of that. I was wrong. In my first moments in the saddle, Bit pulled loose from Ron's grip and tried to walk a nervous circle in the narrow aisle. As I pulled on his reins, Connie reminded me to project calm so that Bit would feel calm. I did my best. And then it was time to go.

As Dud and his accompanist played their final song, I gave Bit a tiny squeeze with my legs – it doesn't take much to get him moving – and we were off. We walked the length of the aisle, and then the few steps into the arena, and then we came abreast of the first big door. That big door was our cue, so I gave Bit another barely-perceptible squeeze. He was meant to break into a trot, then: the routine involved trotting halfway around the arena, then walking the rest of the way before coming to a halt near Duddy. It still would've looked o.k. to the assembled crowd if we had simply walked the whole way around, but Bit trotting would be much cooler! I was prepared for the routine to go either way, but I held out hope as I gave him that squeeze, and what do you know —after hesitating for the briefest of seconds, Bit broke into a trot!

He continued trotting at a stately pace until we reached the big door on the other side of the arena. At that point, I gave a small tug on the reins and he slowed to a walk. We walked a few steps, turned inward toward the wedding party, and then came to a stop.

It was as we were walking those last few steps that I got an unexpected flash of insight from Bit: suddenly, he understood what the training had been about; everything crystallized in his mind with the realization that it had all been for *this*. As we came to a halt, he bobbed his head once, as if to acknowledge the pivotal role he had played, and played so well. I patted him fondly on the neck, told him what a good boy he was, and dismounted.

In ordinary circumstances, that would be the end of Bit's part in the wedding. Indeed, as Ron led him out of the arena, I imagine that everyone thought that that was the last they'd be seeing of him. So it came as a considerable surprise to me when, a few minutes after he disappeared – and after the ceremony had begun – Bit decided to rejoin the party!

I'm not entirely clear on how he managed to break free of Ron's grasp, but at some point while Ron was leading him to a stall, Bit took off at a trot and made his way back into the arena, coming to a stop next to the minister as though he wanted to make sure she was doing her job correctly. It was Wendy who came out and led him away again, and Wendy who remarked later that Bit clearly didn't want to be left out of the proceedings! After seeing the video of it, I'm inclined to agree.

As I took Bit for a walk, a few weeks later, I told him (yet again) what a good boy he was, and how perfectly he had performed on our "special day." I also told him that he'd won a blue ribbon for his effort, which cheered him considerably.

Bit: *A blue ribbon? Really?*

Kelly: "Yep! Because you did so well!"

Bit: *A ribbon for me?*

Kelly: "I'm gonna hang it on your stall door, Bubby!"

Bit: *!!!*

Kelly: "I'm ever so proud of you, Bubby!"

Indeed, Bit's participation in the wedding was the icing on the cake: there could have been no finer wedding for a Critter Lady than one that involved a barn and a horse, as well as the barn cat who walked across the arena in the middle of the ceremony; the photographer actually got a picture of black cat Charlie as he strolled past the bleachers!

I suspect that, as we settled into married life, Duddy might have thought that my interest in animals would wane. He may in fact have hoped that he would replace the critters as my central focus. You can imagine how frustrated he must've been when the realization hit that this would not be the case! Indeed, the way I looked at it was that I now had a partner in crime to assist me, though if I thought he would be enthusiastic about his new role, I turned out to be mistaken!

TEN BUCK DUCK

In my zealous determination to keep my new charges safe, I chased Ethel and Boyfriend Duck around the yard each night, eventually catching them and depositing them in the pen. It was for their own good, but it took me several days to realize that I'd utterly destroyed 8+ years of trust and good-will on their part in the process: chasing them, grabbing them up, and locking them in a pen only served to terrorize them, and once I understood that, I felt *awful*. Unfortunately, there didn't seem to be a way to undo what I'd done, so I set my mind to coming up with *something* – anything – that might fix the problem. The answer finally came to me: another duck.

You can imagine the amount of noise Dud made over the idea of adding a third duck. Two was bad enough, but *three?!* "Do you have any idea what it's going to cost to feed three ducks?" he asked in exasperation, quickly losing patience with me and my ideas.

"A few cents more than it will cost to feed two," I replied evenly. I had anticipated his resistance to the idea, and tried to assure him that grabbing one more duck from the pond wouldn't be any big deal. In truth, I had started out trying to convince him that two more ducks – another male and female – might be the way to go. Then I thought about it and realized that two males would mean territorial disputes every spring, and the need to keep them separate until summer. So I narrowed the plan to just one female duck, someone I easily could catch at McKinnon's pond. *Then* I realized that there weren't any female ducks that I could easily catch at McKinnon's pond!

Unbeknownst to Dud, I went on Craigslist. I entered "Pekin duck" in the search engine, and found that there weren't any locally. The closest domestic duck of any kind was located about forty-five minutes away, and when I emailed the humans involved, they didn't seen particularly certain that they'd be able to catch any of their ducks for me. So I emailed another listing.

The other listing wanted ten bucks per duck. I knew Dud would have a fit about that, too, so I emailed the owners before I said anything. As it turned out, the price wasn't the only thing Dud would have a fit about; the ten buck ducks lived two hours away from Whoville.

"Ten dollars?" he hollered. I'm pretty sure that Russell next door was getting all of this. *"For a duck?! Ten dollars for a duck?! A duck who lives two hours away from our house?"*

"It's a 4-H duck," I replied earnestly, "which means it's been handled by humans and is used to people. We can get a friendly one who will show Ethel and Boyfriend that we're not such horrible people after all!" And, what I didn't say out loud was that driving two hours one way to buy a duck would make a great story for my new book! I let the idea sink in for a day or two, by which time Dud asked me to get on Mapquest to find out how to get to Lucas, Ohio. We then called the duck owners and arranged to drive down and buy a ten buck duck.

If you ignored Dud's swearing, his increasing impatience at what he saw as the highway department's failure to provide concise directional signage, the fact that we got lost a couple of times, *and* the fact that we drove through a valley that provided no cell phone service whatsoever, it was an otherwise pleasant trip. Lucas, as it turned out, was located in a topographically pleasing area of the state – and who knew that Ohio contained anything like that?

We drove the majority of the trip on what William Least Heat Moon referred to as "blue highways" – those one-lane state routes that are mostly devoid of unsightly billboards, ubiquitous fast food joints, and multiple lanes of high-speed traffic – and saw the sort of things you don't ordinarily see much of anymore: roadside fresh vegetable stands that operated on the honor system; snug houses tucked into hillsides, their closest neighbors miles away instead of yards; livestock grazing in verdant pastures. It was all exceedingly fetching.

The duck owner's house was equally fetching. Situated on rolling hills reminiscent of a blanket being shaken and falling gently back into place, the house was clean and tidy. Everything about the place looked cared-for and up-to-date.

Although the property contained a fair-sized pond surrounded by willow trees that lent the scene a charmingly bucolic air, none of the ducks or geese appeared able to use it; their expanse of fenced-in pasture lay some distance away. There were a number of geese, ducks, and chickens in residence. The owner's daughter – Debbie, of the 4-H ducks – joined us outside the pasture fence as we made small talk with her parents, Andy and Sarah. "I don't suppose we can have your favorite duck?" I asked the young girl.

"No," she said, smiling shyly, "but you can have my second-favorite!"

"I want a really *nice*, friendly girl!" I told her.

"O.k.," she said, "I know just the duck!" At which point she proceeded to stalk slowly and methodically around the ducks' pasture until she'd cornered the one she wanted. She tucked the girl under her arm and brought her over for closer inspection. I noted how quickly the duck had calmed down once she'd been caught, and how comfortable she seemed in the girl's arms. "Does she have a name?" I inquired.

"You can call her anything you want," said Debbie.

"In that case," I replied, "her name is Penny Pekin!" The girl smiled as she put Penny in my critter carrier. The girl's mother, Sarah, asked whether we had a proper pen for the ducks. "He built a lovely pen," I answered reassuringly, gesturing toward Dud. What I didn't tell her – and had instructed Duddy not to say, either, was that we weren't using the pen anymore. It remained where we'd set it, but I no longer had the heart to force the ducks into it at night. Instead, I let them stay out in the yard, and hoped like hell that any area predators wouldn't be able to figure a way past the privacy fence. Penny, too, would be free to roam about the yard day and night. We said our good-byes, thanking Debbie for her help, and climbed back into the car.

On the trip home, we inadvertently found ourselves on a major interstate, only this one seemed fairly new, *and* devoid of unsightly billboards and ubiquitous fast food joints. Much to Dud's disgust, before we were too far down the road, Penny managed to poop all over the inside of the carrier. "She's gonna stink up my car!" he moaned.

"Oh, relax," I replied, "it's just a little poop, and it will clear out once we're home."

"Easy for you to say! It's not your car she pooped in!"

"Seriously?" I asked with more than a little irritation, "You seriously think the Critter Lady's never had duck poop in her car? Hell, I've had duck poop on my *clothes!* Quit your bitching!" Which, of course, made him bitch all the more.

"Look," I said through gritted teeth, "you can make this a pleasant trip, or a miserable trip! *Pick one!*" At which point he apologized and cracked his window. The poop smell quickly dissipated.

For her part, Penny appeared to take the unexpected car ride in stride, making only a few squeaky noises of inquiry as we sped toward home. Each time she squeaked, I responded by saying, *"Penny Pekin!"* in a sing-song voice. By the time we got home, two hours later, she seemed to understand that that was her name. When I released her in the yard, she made a beeline toward Ethel and Boyfriend, having, evidently, recognized them as her new best friends.

BUDDY

Half-feral Buddy was twelve years old when Duddy moved in – practically an old man, and (as I thought) set in his ways. I had lived alone for the first eleven years of Bud's life, and I wondered how he would adjust to another presence in the house. Much to my surprise, though, for a cat whose mantra was, "Don't touch me!," he took to Dud almost immediately.

He saw all the extra attention that Spanky was getting, and it's entirely possible that he wanted some for himself. When Duddy would walk into the bedroom to pet Bud, he stayed put, purring happily while Duddy cooed, "Hi Buddy-man! You big handsome man!" Ordinarily, Buddy would only tolerate a few minutes of this sort of thing from me before getting up and repositioning himself a few feet away. I never took it personality – Buddy had his rules, and who was I not to respect them? – but I confess that my nose felt a tiny bit out of joint by Buddy's response to Duddy's attention: affection from me had to be limited, but Duddy could pet him all he wanted?! Honestly!

In spite of his advancing years, Buddy hadn't slowed down much. He still went off on a tear quite regularly, sprinting from one end of the Critter Shack to the other for no apparent reason. He still liked to get stoned out of his mind on catnip, and he still thought of himself as the boss, happily doling out disciplinary smacks to Spanky to put him in his lowly place. And he retained his usual measure of curiosity, poking his investigative nose into things, wanting to be on top of any situation. It was that curiosity that got him into trouble – and Duddy, as well – early on in Dud's Critter Shack residence.

I was forever warning Duddy to make sure that doors were closed – inside the house as well as the outside doors. Because he rarely heeded my warnings, Gracie found herself locked inside the pantry for the better part of an hour before I realized what all her meowing was about and freed her from the closet. I used the experience as a lesson to Duddy, trying to make my point about how easy it was for one of the cats to end up somewhere they weren't meant to be. Even as I said it, though, I could see him mentally dismissing my concern as being a bit over-the-top. Which is how Buddy managed to go outside undetected.

The cats are *never* allowed out unless they're on a leash. The only exception to that rule had died along with gentle, reliable old Muffin. And generally, the cats don't hang around trying to run outside when the door is open, but Buddy saw an opportunity one day that he simply couldn't refuse.

Because I lack a garage, I keep my bicycle in the house, wedged between the dining room table and the window. When I take it outside to ride, I prop the screen door open to facilitate the process. On this occasion, I closed the proper door but left the screen door open as I took off on my ride, knowing that Dud would have the sense to close the proper door behind him when he came home. Upon my return, to my horror, I immediately saw what was wrong: the screen door was still standing open, but now, the proper door was, too. I hollered for Dud the minute I stepped inside.

"What?" he hollered back, wondering what all the fuss was about.

"Did you not see that the screen door was open? Is anyone missing? Have you done a head-count?" I was in a panic while Dud was merely irritated at what he saw as an overreaction on my part – until we came up one cat short. Buddy was unaccounted for. We ran outside.

"Bud? Buddy man? Where's my wild man?" I yelled, looking frantically through the foliage. Because the whole half-acre of property was lushly populated with old-growth landscaping, he could've been anywhere. In addition, I worried about him crossing the street. He didn't understand about traffic, and I seriously doubted that he would know how to find his way home if he wandered too far away.

I began to despair when I heard Dud calling from the side yard, telling me he'd found Buddy under a spirea bush. I made my way over slowly, worried that Buddy would panic at the sight of me running. I walked as quickly but casually as I could, trying to cut him off when he appeared to be heading for the vacant lot next door. Seeing his way blocked, he finally turned toward the house and ran in the door. We followed him in, and then I gave Dud The Look. You know the one, the one that says, "If you *ever* fuck up like that again, *I will have your balls on a silver platter!*" Dud tried to pretend that he didn't know what The Look meant.

Happily for me and my cat, Buddy seemed none the worse for wear, even if his curiosity about the outside world *had* been piqued. I knew then that I would have to be extra-vigilant in the future, because from then on, Buddy was going to be extra nosy around open doors.

CONVERSATIONS
WITH MY HORSE

I've never claimed to be an animal communicator – and I'm not sure whether I believe in them or not – but I think that just about anyone who has a pet will agree that as the bond between you grows, the ability to understand your pet does, too. In my first book, *Crazy Critter Lady*, I made it clear that while the animals around me do, in fact, communicate with me, it's not the sort of talking that humans do with flapping lips and wagging tongues. Indeed, it's more like an understanding of the gist of that critter's thoughts. And I have to say that some of those thoughts can be real doozies!

My pal Bit is a great example of this. Bit doesn't say a heck of a lot, but when he does, it gives me pause for thought. One of our more memorable exchanges took place while we were walking along the track outside the fence. All but three of his herd were busy doing their thing inside the fence. The three in question were old fellows, geezers, really. Combined, they had almost ninety years of life behind them. They were in the far corner of the mud lot, away from the action: Keeper, Newman, and E.T., shoulder to shoulder, standing quietly, tails swishing the odd fly away. They would remain motionless in the hot sun for some time. Gesturing in their direction, I said to Bit, "You'll be one of them one day, Bubby!" Meaning that one day, he'd be an old motionless geezer, too. But he heard my words differently and replied, *No, Kelly, I'll always be me!* His logic was unassailable, even if he *had* missed my point.

Another time, as we walked up the driveway, he announced, out of nowhere, *I don't like your hair.* I'd had it cut recently, and it was considerably shorter than it had been the last time he'd seen me. "Why?" I asked, mystified. *It's different,* was his inarguable response, which served to reinforce in my mind the notion that Bit prefers consistency. I'd had no idea that something as inconsequential as a haircut would upset his sense of balance, but there it was, literally straight from the horse's mouth.

While I believe wholeheartedly in the idea that the animals around me share their thoughts with me from time to time, I'm a confirmed skeptic when it comes to the idea of animal communicators. I'd tried one or two and had not been bowled over by what they had to say. Barn owner Wendy, though, put great stock in an animal communicator that she knew, and hosted the woman at the barn at more or less regular intervals. Mildly intrigued by the possibilities, I put my name on the board where Wendy announced that Davinia would be holding fifteen-minute sessions with whoever wanted them. I was keen to see whether Bit had anything to say that I didn't already know. I texted Mandy with the news, knowing that she would have something to say about it, but she waited until after the event took place to share her thoughts.

Dud wasn't the least bit happy when he found out that this particular hokum was going to cost $30.00. "Don't worry," I said, by way of reassurance, "I'll pay for it out of my greeter money!"

"*Yeah, you will!*" he replied a bit more forcefully than was necessary. Privately, I hoped that the session would be worth what it was going to cost me.

I asked relatively few questions of Davinia. If she was so good at this mind-reading stuff, then she'd already know what I was wondering about, right? As it turned out, the session did not go as I'd expected. In the first place, Bit didn't appear to have a lot on his mind. There were issues of pain from old injuries, and suggestions that I learn to relax more in the saddle and have a better seat. But beyond that, Bit seemed, on the whole, fairly satisfied with our relationship. At the very least, he didn't seem *unhappy* with it. I came away from the session feeling as skeptical as I was going in. I'd been neither convinced of her talents nor disabused of their existence.

"Is Bit mentally disturbed?" came Mandy's text later that day.

"No, but I am!" was my obvious reply.

"I already knew that," she answered.

One of the regular themes of my conversations with Bit, a subject we would return to many times in the course of our relationship, was the fact of his skittishness. Bit was so nervous, he jumped at *everything*: hoses, tree branches, barn cats, the wind – you name it, it scared him. When I shared my observations with Wendy, she decided to put him on an herbal supplement. I was privately skeptical; I'd been on some supplements myself and couldn't see a lick of difference in my overall health. Time would tell whether they'd have any effect on Bit.

Bit only really startled when I took him out of his comfort zone. The driveway, the track outside the pasture, these were new places for him, with foreign sounds and smells. While I could be a little jumpy in strange situations, too, my being startled didn't involve running nervous circles around a creature much smaller than me. When Bit startled, he was throwing a thousand pounds-worth of weight around, and whether he trampled me in the process wasn't something he worried about. As riding instructor Connie told me, it was my job to keep calm in such situations, rather than feed into Bit's fear. That was easier said than done when I had no idea what had frightened him, or how he was going to react this time, but I did my best to set an example of calm for Bit and over time, it seemed to help. Even so, he never completely lost his fear of new things.

"Bubby, you're not *meant* to be afraid of *everything*!" I told him.

It's my job, Kelly! came the emphatic reply. What he meant was, it was his job to know what constituted a threat to his herd, so that he could keep them safe. Unfortunately, he tended to take things a little too far, so that even the most benign object ended up being suspect. That level of vigilance required what must have been an exhausting amount of energy on his part.

The most disconcerting talk Bit and I shared took place as winter tightened its frigid grip on Whoville. The entire country had been swathed in an arctic blast of epic proportions: snow fell in record amounts from west to east all across the country, accompanied by devastating wind chills in the minus degrees. In that sort of weather, there was not much that Bit and I could do: it was much too blowy and snowy to go outside, and it was too cold in the arena to do anything more than walk Bit around on a lead rope because Wendy didn't want anyone riding when the temperature was below 25 degrees.

Her concern had to do with stiff equine muscles not getting properly warmed up or cooled down, during a ride, and she worried about horses getting pneumonia in such drastic cold, as well. This left us with very little else to do. I'd already trained him for the wedding, and he'd performed admirably. Now, I was at a loss for fun winter ways to keep us occupied. Happily, one of the barn volunteers raised the subject of riding bareback – a thing Bit and I had never done. I got the go-ahead to try from Wendy and hopped up on Bit's bare back a few days later.

He immediately tried to throw me off. Every time I try something that he doesn't feel like doing, Bit will do a little mini buck and rear. He never really gets airborne; he only ever throws his weight around just enough to get the idea across. And that first time on his back, I got the message loud and clear that he did *not* like this new thing! He pulled the same stunt the second time I rode him, too. By the third ride, I'd had enough of his protests. All we were doing was walking in circles in the arena. No trotting, no loping, and no uncomfortable girth tightened around his midsection. Just walking. When he reared yet again on the third ride, I told him firmly, "You can buck all you want, Bit, but I'm not going anywhere!!"

Bit: *I don't like this, Kelly!*

Kelly: "We have to learn how to do it, Bubby."

Bit: *I already know how!* He repeatedly flailed his head up and down to emphasize his point.

Kelly: "You might know, but *I* need to learn."

Bit: *Learn faster!*

I couldn't believe it! *"Seriously?!* That's your answer? 'Learn faster'?" Wow! A horse with absolutely no patience, and no sympathy, either!

Bit: *!!!*

Kelly: "You're no help at all, Bubby! I'm patient with you! The least you can do is be patient with me!"

Bit: *But Kelly! It's <u>boring</u>!*

Kelly: "Live with it, Bit! It won't kill you!"

Bit: *hmmmph!*

The conversation brought home to me how intelligent Bit is, and how hard it is for me to keep his mind occupied with challenging things. Bit reckons, if I'm going to take him away from his herd duties, I should at least make it interesting for him. That's not an easy thing to do: Bit knows much more than I do about horsemanship, training, and competing. Even when I set up an obstacle course for him, I have to change it up more than once, during our ride, because he figures it out so quickly. And once Bit figures something out, he doesn't want to do it anymore. Only the occasional threat will prod him onward.

"We will be riding like this," I announced in my I'm-the-boss voice, "until *I* say we're done! So I suggest that you straighten up and fly right, mister! No more bucking! Or else!" Bit didn't know what the "or else!" entailed, but given the tone of voice I used, it was clear that he didn't want to push his luck and find out. In the meantime, I needed to consult Connie and get some suggestions as to how to keep Bit busy and challenged during the dreary winter months ahead, before he *really* got impatient.

Over time, Duddy seemed to settle into the idea that critters would play a prominent role in our marriage. When I mentioned that I thought we should put up some netting to discourage area hawks from trying to attack the ducks, Dud merely nodded and asked for details, rather than do his usual ten-minute rant about the cost of keeping ducks. Slowly but surely, I think he began to understand that without the critters, I wouldn't be the person he'd fallen in love with. Still, acceptance did not come easily.

WORMS!

While Ethel and Boyfriend continued to maintain their reserve, Penny Pekin was the complete opposite: she nattered happily every time we so much as stuck our heads out the back door, and waddled excited circles around us when we went out to feed her. She made a variety of squeaky noises, quacking so loudly that I'm certain poor Russell next door could hear, and generally wormed her way into our hearts quite quickly.

Duddy complained frequently about the rising cost of keeping the ducks – we had added an in-ground pond when they'd refused to use the children's wading pool we'd bought, a project that grew to include not just the plastic pond liner but also several bags of decorative stone, and multiple bags of mulch – and his complaints reached a fevered pitch when I discovered the bait shop located just across the river from Whoville.

It was my mother who had mentioned Shoney's bait shop. Having availed herself of its worms when she'd been composting, she informed me that they stocked a healthy supply of just the sort of thing I'd been looking for to supplement the ducks' diet of cracked corn and game-bird pellets. Two dozen large nightcrawlers could be had for $3.99. I made a beeline for Shoney's!

"We can't afford to keep buying them worms all the time," Dud announced.

"Why not? They're not that expensive, and you see how much the ducks love them!" Indeed, the ducks were so enthusiastic about the addition to their diet that they would actually try to steal them out of each other's bills. Penny was the worst offender in this regard, and gimpy Boyfriend was no match for her fleet feet. We learned the hard way that we had to toss Penny's worm some distance away and then quickly toss one directly to Boyfriend if he was to stand any chance of enjoying them.

"I'm not spending good money on *worms for ducks!*" was his emphatic reply. But Dud was worse than I was about doling out the delicacy: any number of times on a given day, I would walk into the family room to find him on his way into the back yard, container of worms in hand. "Penny Pekin!" he'd croon, copying my sing-song voice, *"I've got worms!"* I would give him The Look as he walked back in the house, the look that says *who are you kidding, here, worm-giver?!* He would try to insist that he hadn't handed out that many, but "that many" was a relative term.

The guy at Shoney's quickly came to recognize me, and made a point of telling me, on several different visits, that the shop would be closed for the month of November. This was disastrous news because I had expanded my purchase to include minnows as well as worms. Nothing delighted Ethel and Penny more than when I dumped a few dozen minnows into their water bucket. Racing over as fast as their feet would carry them, they bobbed happily until every last minnow was gone, a task that usually took no more than three or four minutes to accomplish. They ate them so fast that slow-poke Boyfriend could never get to the bucket in time to eat any himself. Their joy was palpable and slightly addictive, to boot. What we would do when we ran out of treats in November was beyond me, so without telling Duddy, I loaded up on supplies. I brought the six containers home and tried to hide them in the back of the refrigerator, but Dud found them later the same day.

"You bought six containers of worms?" he asked in disbelief. There was no point in denying it, as I clearly *had* bought six containers, so I simply joined him in staring at the inside of the fridge in consternation. He looked at the fridge, and then looked at me, waiting, evidently, for an explanation. He knew about the bait shop closing in November as well as I did, so I did no more than return his gaze. He repeated the question.

"I heard you the first time," I answered, "I just didn't think a response was necessary."

"You paid over thirty-five dollars for worms," he stated.

"I did, indeed, and boy, is Penny going to be thrilled!" I enthused. It would not be the last time that Dud sighed in resignation and murmured to himself, "it's only money!"

Ethel and Boyfriend may have been reserved, but they learned to follow Penny's lead when it came to getting treats. If Penny made a beeline for the patio, the other two would be hot on her heels, determined to get their fair share of whatever was being doled out. Since Ethel and Boyfriend had eaten nothing but bugs, worms, and the corn I fed them at McKinnon's pond, they turned up their bills at any other offerings. Penny, on the other hand, was raised on a farm where fruit and vegetables were regular diet staples, which meant that she happily tackled both tomatoes and watermelon. Her breakfast each morning came to be a dish of diced tomatoes while Ethel and Boyfriend enjoyed two worms apiece.

Whenever all three ducks wandered onto the patio, I rewarded their bravery with worms. They came to learn that if they stopped by for a visit, there were snacks in it for them, and Penny, especially, was encouraged to hop up on the back step – and ultimately take a step inside the house – to retrieve a juicy worm snack. She would stand on that step hesitantly, torn between coming in for the worm, and playing it safe, given that at least one cat was usually in the family room watching. She chose the worm almost every time. She would step inside, snatch her prize, and then head quickly out the door. Neither Ethel nor Boyfriend would even consider doing such a thing, maintaining as they did a resolute distance about half-way across the patio.

It was because of those patio visits, and Dud's daily offerings in the yard, that we raced through that supply of worms all too quickly, running out before we were halfway through November. In a mild panic, I searched for bait shops online, eventually finding one nearby. "Would you pick up some worms at Boatman's Paradise?" I asked Dud over the phone. When he came home later complaining about the price, I thought *are we really going to have this discussion again?* But I said nothing, knowing, as I did, that I would eventually catch him doling out generous portions to what were fast becoming not just *my* pet ducks, but *his*, too.

JUNEBUG

While I have a sneaking suspicion that I'm expected to love all four of my cats equally, that is not the case. While I do love them all *individually*, I actually love Junebug the most. Since the day I brought her home as a kitten, ten years ago, we've shared an unshakeable bond that transcends the usual pet/owner relationship.

Junebug became my favorite because, while the other cats chose to keep their emotional distance from me, she actively sought out my company. Even now, as she did then, Junebug will follow me to the bathroom, intent on enjoying some lap time while I'm sitting down. In the evenings, she follows me in again to keep me company while I brush my teeth and wash my face. She's come to learn that if she waits patiently enough on the bath mat, I will eventually get down on all fours and snuggle with her. That's not the only time I'm on the floor with her.

Because her favorite hobby is kibble, Junebug spends a lot of time lying on the kitchen floor, waiting for someone to top off the food bowl. More often than not, I'll lie down on the floor with her, petting her and calling her all of the nicknames I've come up with for her over the years: Little Mitten, Junebug Gem, Honey Bee, etc. She never seems to tire of the attention. Many times, she'll announce, *I love you, Kelly!* and I, of course, will reply, "I love you, too, Mit!"

We've developed a morning routine, in our time at the Critter Shack, in which I sit down to breakfast at the table and open the pantry door which is just behind my chair. Junebug will go into the pantry and wander among the boots – most of them smelling wondrously of horse barn and horse poop – and she will roll around ecstatically, happily absorbing the smells while she waits for me to finish eating. Once I'm done, it's time to break out the cat treats.

The game goes like this: Junebug stands on one side of the pantry door, and I crouch on the other, sliding treats under the door and across the floor for her to chase and eat. She's always very enthusiastic about this game, running this way and that, chasing her snack treats around the floor. It's a daily ritual that we both enjoy. We sometimes play a similar game with toy mice because Junebug still has enough energy, in spite of her girth, to enjoy dashing about like a younger cat.

She's picked up an unfortunate bullying habit over the years, aimed primarily at Gracie, who is truly a benign little soul that doesn't bother anyone, though I suspect that it has to do with Gracie's limp, which tends to render her vulnerable to such attacks. If Gracie's not around and Junebug feels cranky, she'll turn her bitchiness on Spanky and give him a few smacks until I intervene. I don't like this sort of behavior and try to discourage it as best I can.

Duddy doesn't like such behavior either, and while he's nice to Junebug, and croons sweetly to her while he pets her, he finds her bullying vexing and firmly remonstrates her whenever she starts picking on someone. I think that she's

Dud's least favorite cat, but that's o.k. because she gets more than enough attention from me.

After all these years, our nightly ritual continues to be a source of joy for me. For as long as I can remember, Junebug has spent at least some part of every night snuggled next to my pillow. Sometimes, she'll bring a toy mouse up with her, purring happily as she settles down to sleep. There are times, too, when she doesn't join me until the wee hours of the morning, waking me in the process because she's just heaved eighteen pounds of cat up next to my pillow. Finding her purring too irresistible to ignore, I'll groggily pet her for a few minutes before falling back to sleep.

If I've learned nothing else from the heartache I experienced after Muffin's death, I've learned this: that our time together is all too brief, and should not be taken for granted. Which is why I've made a concerted effort, in the time since Muff's passing, to liberally sprinkle my affections on all four cats every single day.

Each day, I make a point of spending a little quality time with each cat, whether it be handing out snacks, cuddling for a few minutes, petting and head-butts, or playing with toys. And while I'm at it, you can believe that I'm trying mightily to memorize all those important features for when they're no longer here: the sound of Junebug's purr; the wide-eyed look on Spanky's face just before we butt heads; the way Gracie drools happily when I pet her; and how Buddy always smells curiously like a corn chip.

I already know that the thing I will miss most about Junebug is our discussions. We chat on a daily, sometimes hourly, basis. Much of our talk centers on my assertion that she has "rabbity feet." Junebug, like every other cat I've known, takes exception to this: she always corrects me, stating firmly that, *I'm a cat, Kelly! I have cat feet!* To mess with her, I respond by telling her that while cats have rabbit feet, rabbits have cat feet. She's not buying it. She does, however, lap it up when I tell her that she's Momma's Little Mitten, the cutest kitty in all the land.

In spite of her advancing years, Junebug still likes to play. She particularly enjoys kicking around the catnip toys that my seamstress friend Dolores and I make every year with my home-grown catnip. Other times, she'll bat at a toy mouse, and it's not uncommon for her to carry one around in her mouth, usually with a view to giving it to me so that we might play with it. When I lie in bed at night hearing a strange sort of *Owww? Rrrowww?* noise coming from the hallway, I know that it's Junebug trying to meow with a toy mouse in her mouth, asking me to play.

Junebug does a lot of asking, which has to do mostly with food bowl top-off requests. Junebug is a big fan of kibble (hence her sizeable girth), but she's an even bigger fan of *fresh* kibble, the kind that doesn't smell of another cat's slobber. If Dud or I are in the house, she'll ask repeatedly for fresh kibble. Naturally, when no one's home, she'll eat what's there. More often than not, Dud and I will ignore the first few rounds of meowing, hoping that she'll give up and eat what's already in the bowl. Sometimes, though, it turns out she's not meowing about kibble.

I can recall an evening when I was still living at the chicken coop. I was in the living room reading and Junebug kept calling to me from the hallway. I did my best to ignore her for ten minutes or so before giving in and walking out into the hallway. It turned out that it wasn't a kibble request at all, but rather Junebug asking for my help.

For whatever reason, the chicken coop played host to an astonishing number of very large spiders – creatures that do *not* enjoy the dedicated protection of the Critter Lady. This particular evening, Junebug had been trying to make a meal out of a particularly muscular arachnid – think Black Widow

on steroids – without much success. The thing simply refused to die, no matter that Junebug was a hundred times
bigger than it was. I think she managed to injure it, but even
so, the spider wasn't backing down; it continued to hold its
own in the middle of the hallway. Horrified, I grabbed one
of those big, hard-cover coffee table books that you see in
Architectural Digest and dropped it directly on the creature.
While the falling book managed to kill the thing, it wasn't
able to flatten it: the corpse was still three-dimensional.
Junebug refused to eat it; she simply wanted to make sure
that it was dead.

She seems to have lost her passion for bug eating at the
Critter Shack. Every now and then, I'll encourage her to eat
a dead fly – mostly to save me from having to pick it up and
dispose of it – and most times, she'll take a pass. Bugs don't
seem to hold the attraction that they once did. Strangely,
though, she has a peculiar fondness for eating toilet paper. I
have no idea why.

She actually caught a live mouse, once. It was the winter
that I had been feeding the house mice, then humanely trap-
ping and releasing them, only to have them come right back
in the house again. It was a naive humanitarian effort that
got way out of hand, given my lack of understanding about
the tenacity of house mice. When Duddy first moved in, they
were still lurking about in the cupboards and he was horrified to learn that I'd actually been feeding them. He refused
to share the house with them and, knowing that I did not
want to be responsible for a mass mousicide, he took matters
into his own hands with the understanding that I would go
along with it, but did *not* want anything to do with the details. Suffice to say that the house is now mouse-free.

In any case, Junebug had somehow caught a mouse – and
who knew that she could manage such a thing, being quite fat
and extremely lazy? – and just in time, I noticed her carrying

it across the kitchen floor. When I called out, "Hey!," she dropped the little fellow, who immediately rolled onto his back and – I swear this is true – put up both his little forepaws like a boxer in the ring, as though he was going to try to knock her out if she came at him again. Junebug had no idea what to make of that but I saw it for the opportunity it was, leaned over and picked the little guy up. I let him go in the field next door to the Shack. Junebug didn't seem to hold it against me. I don't think she had any real idea of what to do with a live mouse anyway.

I tried teaching her to walk on a leash the previous summer. The idea of walking her around the yard, burning a few cat calories, seemed like a good one. Much to my surprise, though, Junebug was genuinely afraid to go outside. I was mystified. Buddy and Spanky never needed much encouragement to go for walks, but Junebug refused to leave the safety of the brick patio, preferring instead to roll around on her back and chew on the various weeds growing up between the bricks. I decided to try again the following spring when, as I like to tell her, the breezes bring the smells right to her nose. Someday, I hope she'll embrace the outings with the same measure of glee that the boys do. Until then, I'll continue tossing treats to my Little Mitten – it's the only real exercise she gets.

THE DUCK I DIDN'T SAVE

It was not uncommon to run across Animal Control Officer Dave as he made his rounds in Whoville. Indeed, Duddy and I noticed his crittering truck stopped in the middle of the road one day as we finished up feeding the McKinnon's Pond ducks. He had been talking to someone – everyone in town knew him – and stayed put when he saw us approach. Dud, a roofing contractor, had done some work for Dave years ago; Whoville was a small world unto itself. We greeted him, and then chatted briefly, but Dave appeared to be a man with things on his mind. "You have bad news for me, don't you?" I asked accusingly. Dave nodded, but the bad news was not what I was expecting.

I had recently emailed Jon Watson, Whoville's Director of Important Things, asking when he thought the McKinnon's Pond fountain might be turned on for the winter. Jon was the guy who'd been keeping the fountain running for a number of years, now, and if it weren't for him, the domestic ducks would have died quite some time ago. This year, though, I hadn't heard back from Jon and I feared the worst.

But Officer Dave wasn't bearing bad fountain news. He was bearing bad duck news. "You know that pond over in the Willow Crest subdivision?" he asked. I looked at him askance; I knew where the Willow Crest subdivision was, but I'd had no idea that they had their own pond. "They've got a pond?" I asked in surprise.

"Yes, and someone dumped a white duck in it. Apparently it was a school project," he added.

"We really need to do something about those school projects," I interjected.

"Mmmm," he said, noncommittally, "well, I went over to try and catch it but couldn't get near the thing. I was going to call you and see if you'd go have a look."

"We'll check it out this week," I promised.

The Willow Crest subdivision was a rather moneyed neighborhood, the houses large and tidy with plenty of old-growth landscaping. Even though I'd grown up in Whoville, I'd never had any reason to go to that particular subdivision, so the fact of a private pond was news to me. Dud knew the way, though, and parked near the common area, a small hill with a shelter and fire pit, and tennis courts next door for the use of the Crest residents.

The pond was a small one, with two aerators and a raft floating in the middle. I saw no sign of the Pekin but she saw us from her vantage point in a resident's yard and made a beeline for the water. She didn't stop swimming until she'd reached the raft and floated next to it, watching us the whole time. Instinctively, I knew that this was going to be a complicated rescue. I left the Crest disheartened.

I chewed on the situation for more than a week before I called Dave back. "I have a couple of ideas to run by you," I told him.

"O.k.," he replied.

"The first is, if you're agreeable, I can write a letter to the *Whoville Journal*, asking the person who dumped the duck to call me if they can catch her, and I'll come pick her up, no questions asked. The second is, is the Crest association going to leave those aerators on all winter?"

"No," Dave said, "they told me they'd be turning them off."

"Rats! Well, there goes that idea!"

"I like the letter-to-the-paper idea," Dave replied. "Meanwhile, I've got a friend who lives there, and his property backs up to the pond. *And* he's got a fence! I was thinking we could herd the duck inside his fence and then capture it."

"Great idea," I answered, "but the minute that duck saw me, it made a beeline for the pond, so we're probably going to need boats and extra bodies." Neither of us was particularly taken by the idea of boats chasing ducks around a pond. "We've got some time before winter hits, why don't we see if the letter works, and put your idea on the back burner for later?"

"Sounds like a plan," Dave said and hung up. The *Journal* printed my letter the following week. A day later, the woman who dumped the duck called me.

"I didn't know she couldn't fly when I agreed to take her," the woman said.

"Do you think you can catch her?" I asked.

"I'm pretty sure my son can. And I have a place I can take her to."

"O.k. Feel free to call me if you need any extra people to help you." She said she would, and I relayed the conversation to Dave. We agreed to wait and see what happened.

Meanwhile, Dud and I went out canvassing for jobs. Dud has me drive around various Whoville neighborhoods while he checks out the roofs. When he finds one that looks old, he knocks on the door and offers to give the residents a free estimate. This particular day, I happened to park the car directly across from the driveway of one Aimee Van Staten.

I knew Aimee from rescue circles: not only did her road-kill shoveling rival my own, but Aimee was also the founder and president of Critter Fix, Whoville's low-cost spay/neuter clinic, serving seven counties in NW Ohio and SE Michigan. Aimee had worked for the Whoville Humane Society, Best Friends Animal Society, *and* the ASPCA. Like me, she was hardcore for critters! And she was just getting out of her car when I pulled over to park. "Hey!" she called, "what brings you here?"

"My new husband does roofing," I told her.

"He does *what?*" she asked as she walked toward me.

"Roofing. He does roofing."

"Are you serious?" she asked incredulously. "I'm in dire need of a roof! And so is the clinic!" I called Dud over. As we walked around to the back of her house, I mentioned the dumped Willow Crest duck. "Aww!" she said, "I hate when people do that!"

"You and me both," I remarked, "and she's going to be a real challenge to catch, too." I gave her the details as Dud studied the roof line. He told her he'd come back with his ladder, and promised to check out the roof at Critter Fix, too. We parted company, then, and Dud and I continued canvassing.

"I can't stop thinking about the Willow Crest duck!" read the email I got from Aimee several days later. She said she had a friend who specialized in these sorts of rescues, and told me he would be coming to town in a couple of weeks.

"Great!" I enthused, "maybe you could ask him to help?" Aimee promised that she would. The next time I heard from her, though, she sounded like she was going to attempt the rescue herself.

"Let me know if you need extra bodies," I emailed in response.

"This is your area of expertise," she answered, "I'm happy to defer to you."

"Not at all," I replied, "you're not stepping on any toes here. If you have a plan, by all means, go for it!" And she did just that. While I was busy procrastinating, Aimee had organized a couple of boats and a couple of people, all of whom managed to not only herd the Pekin onto dry land, but into a fenced yard, as well. With a towel, she caught the duck – her very first duck rescue ever – and trundled it off to a carefully-vetted new home. I was never even called in to assist them. *Great!* I thought, *now I don't have to be the only duck rescuer in Whoville!* But that thought was followed closely by another, more troubling one: duck rescues were my domain; why didn't I help? It's what I do. It's what I'm known for. *What was I thinking?!* I suddenly felt very off-kilter.

I took the matter to my therapist. "I don't like this feeling at all," I told her.

"So you passed one up," she shrugged. "How many rescues have you done – *all by yourself* – over the years?" She had a point.

"Yeah, but this is my *identity*," I replied. "What will people think? That the Duck Lady has retired?"

"The people who know you, know better," she said firmly. "Passing up one duck rescue doesn't mean that you're out of the game." Dud said more or less the same thing when I brought it up with him. "There's no reason you should be the only rescuer in Whoville," he remarked. Reluctantly, I agreed.

I sent Aimee an email, congratulating her on the rescue and apologizing for what I called a "bit of critter burnout" on my part. As a fellow rescuer, I knew she understood, even if I didn't: ordinarily, I was right on top of these things. This time, though, I delayed and procrastinated, putting things off for a vague, indeterminate amount of time. I don't know what I had been hoping, other than for the woman who originally dumped him to actually catch him and save me the trouble. I knew this much: my overall energy for these things was waning, and I found that puzzling.

When I turned the matter over in my mind, though, I was surprised to realize that I'd been in the rescue game for well over ten years, now. Thirteen years of life and death, of health emergencies and heartache, of personal expense and emotional energy, all without a break. It was enough to burn anyone out. I made the decision, then, to relax a little, let go a little, *breathe,* slow down, and, once in a while, ask for help. It would be the only way to keep doing what I'd been doing all these years.

Lest anyone think that mine will be a happily-ever-after story, let me point out that mental illness is <u>manageable</u>, but not <u>curable</u>. I'm always a little frightened by how fast and easy it is to go from relative sanity to completely unhinged: one minute, I'm being fairly reasonable, and the next, I'm jumping off the precipice with the bottom nowhere in sight. My friend Lynnette has a term for it: bat shit crazy.

BAT SHIT CRAZY

While Lynnette always used the term with a certain affection, it must be said that she had no idea how close to the mark she was. My main difficulty stemmed from a total inability to deal with conflict. What for normal people would require little more than a few "*fuck you*'s" followed by a few "*I'm sorry*'s" was completely beyond me. When Dud and I wrangled, I inevitably found myself in the midst of a big black hole that was nearly impossible to get out of.

There was nothing in that black hole. No thought, no feeling, just a numbness that enveloped me like a blanket. Anger and sadness would come later, but initially, it was like Maxwell Smart's Cone of Silence: nothing could get in, and nothing could get out. It was a kind of insanity that I'd been on intimate terms with for decades, but that no one else could possibly understand unless they, too, were bat shit crazy.

There was one particularly memorable incident. We'd been arguing over something I can no longer recall, when the switch flipped in my head, and I suddenly found myself in that black place. I drove off in my car, destination unknown. All I knew at that point was that I didn't want to go home. Ever. So I occupied myself reading trashy magazines at the public library. When my interest in that flagged, I made my way back to my car and sat, in the dark, in the library parking lot, staring mindlessly out the windshield. Two words were in my head: *suicide* and *hospital*. I gave each equal consideration.

As for *suicide*, I couldn't decide on a method. The problem with attempting to kill yourself is that Hollywood makes it look incredibly easy. I can tell you from personal experience that it is *not*. The human body seems to have a built-in mechanism for survival, and barring a loaded gun, or Dr. Kevorkian, at your disposal, the remaining options are very difficult to pull off.

As for *hospital*, the psyche ward is a nice place to visit, but, like the electric fence at The Harmony Barn, you really don't want to experience it twice. The one thing hospitalization at St. Stephen's had going for it was good food, which is always a bonus, and a decent occupational therapy program. I just wasn't entirely sure I was ready for a 72-hour lockdown. Which made calling my therapist after hours my only other option. But I wasn't quite ready for that, yet, either.

So I continued to stare mindlessly out the windshield until the library closed. Then I drove to an all-night grocery store and parked. I stared mindlessly out the windshield there, too, for a time. Finally, lacking any other ideas on where to spend the rest of the evening, I drove home and sat, staring mindlessly out the windshield, in my own driveway. I was not inclined to go inside.

At some point in the small hours of the night, I remembered that I had a Hudson Bay blanket stashed in the trunk. Once I'd wrapped that around me, I settled in fairly comfortably and fell asleep. A couple hours later, I was awakened by

Dud peering in the window and asking, "What the fuck are you doing?" "Sleeping," I replied, turning away from him. He went back inside without further comment.

I went in the house the next morning. Words were exchanged. "Sleeping in your car *in your own driveway* is *not normal!*" he ranted. "Welcome to bat shit crazy," I replied evenly, "are you staying or leaving?" I broke down, crying, shortly after that. While I felt a huge measure of empathy for Dud – who had signed on for this relationship knowing only that there was a rather vague mental illness issue, and had ended up with a part-time lunatic instead – I felt much worse for myself: that big black hole was getting bigger, and closer, and easier to fall into, and harder to get out of, and I found that fact far more disturbing than the idea of sleeping in my car. It was time to call the therapist.

She could squeeze me in for thirty minutes at the end of the day, she said. I took it. Hunched up on her couch (yes, she really does have one, along with a recliner and a couple of uncomfortable-looking chairs), hugging a decorative pillow to my chest, I shared my concern about the size and shape of that black hole. She suggested a change of medication, an idea I pooh-poohed: all my previous forays into the world of psychotropic drugs had proved disastrous. I experienced just about every possible side-effect there was, until it finally seemed easier to go without. Still, the idea was not without merit.

That evening, Dud and I snuggled on the bed and discussed the matter further. The only drug I'd tried that actually worked, I told him, was Prozac.

"Why did you go off it?" he wanted to know.

"Because those drugs steal your soul," I replied. "There are no lows, but there are no highs, either, and that flat-line feeling isn't natural; you're meant to feel things. So I went off it."

Dud thought about that for a minute. "I can live with flat-line if you can," he said, "why don't you try it and see how it goes this time?" As much for him as for myself, I agreed.

As luck would have it, I already had an appointment scheduled with the Whoville County mental health entity that oversaw my medications. I told the nurse what I had in mind: another attempt at using an anti-depressant to combat the meltdowns that were happening more often. She agreed that it might be a good idea, and wrote me a prescription. "Come back in a month and tell me how you're doing," she said as I left. I filled the scrip that same day.

Apart from two day's-worth of increased anxiety early on, the Prozac appeared to do its job. Over the next few weeks, I noticed that I seemed calmer, less volatile. It wasn't a dramatic change, but then, that's not how anti-depressants work anyway. It's more of a subtle, gradual change, more an *absence* of symptoms rather than an *addition* of mood. That may not make sense to the layman, but I'd bet money that anyone who's ever taken a psychotropic drug will understand perfectly.

While the Prozac seemed to be helping, there was still the issue of the added stresses in my life taking their toll. Stressor #1 was my new husband. We'd lived together for a year before we got married, but the Critter Shack is a small place, and I'd yet to get used to having another person there with me 24/7. Space was at a premium, and there was no way to have any quiet time to myself without actually leaving the house. There was no question but that I would learn to adjust, though, so that meant dealing with Stressor #2 – the greeter gig.

I had taken a month-long leave of absence from my job in order to deal with the new medication in my system. My thinking was that if I began to experience any of the usual side effects – increased anxiety, dizziness, suicidal thoughts – I would be dealing with them in the safety of my own home, rather than on the clock at work. And, it was conceivable that I could be fired for working under the influence of a drug. So I took the time off and put it to good use getting things done around the house. But the job was never far from my thoughts.

On the one hand, I quite liked the job, and the people I worked with. Being a greeter was relatively easy, there wasn't much in the way of managerial supervision breathing down my neck, and I enjoyed chatting with the regular customers. On the other hand, there had been a change in leadership, which meant a change in scheduling, and I didn't care for the new boss *or* the new schedule. In addition, even though I'd worked the job for over a year, I still found it emotionally taxing: when you live with depression and the desire for isolation that comes with it, having to be somewhere on a regular basis, and having to deal with other human beings in the bargain, can be very tiring. In theory, the Prozac would relieve me of the burden of anxiety I felt during every shift, but I wasn't sure I wanted to bother with the job anymore.

"Thinking about quitting the greeter gig," I texted Mandy.

"Why?" she texted back.

"Humans are exhausting," I replied.

"You only work two days a week!" she responded incredulously.

"I know! And it takes five days to recover!"

"You're ridiculous," she informed me.

"It's not easy being me!" was my inarguable answer. Ultimately, I decided to give up the job in the hope that the decrease in stress would decrease the level of bat shit crazy.

❄

WINTER WAYS

I knew I was in trouble the first time the garden hose froze. I needed that hose to convey water, not just to top off the ducks' pond, but to refill their water bucket, and hose down all the poops, as well. And I would need that free-flowing water all winter. The early freeze in mid-November had me scrambling for ideas on how to make my daily duck chores easier through the cold months, but I dreaded telling Duddy because I knew what he'd say.

"You want *what?*" he asked incredulously, when I finally mentioned my idea. "After all the money I've spent on *your* ducks, you want me to spend more?!"

I looked at him askance. "I beg your pardon...*whose* ducks are they?"

He peered at me over his glasses. "Right now, they're *yours!*"

"Let's just go to Nelson's and see what they've got," I implored him. Later that day, we drove over to the "Save Big Bucks" DIY store and wandered around the mostly-deserted garden center. Nelson's had a lot of cheap stuff on offer, and

I hoped that what I wanted would be cheap enough to make Dud agreeable to its purchase.

What I wanted was this: a hose caddy on wheels, the kind with a spool that you wind the hose around. "Why can't you just roll up the hose on your arm and bring it in the house each night?" Dud wanted to know.

"All one hundred feet of it?" I countered, giving him the *what, are you nuts?* look. There was no way I was going to haul one hundred feet of hose into the house every evening and plop it on the laundry room floor to ooze water all night long.

"*Twenty-five bucks for a hose caddy?*" he howled in out-rage when he read the price tag. Dud could be a really gener-ous soul – *most* of the time. Other times, though, he could be a total cheapskate, and there, in the middle of Nelson's garden center, he chose to be a cheapskate. I sighed and said nothing, figuring he'd come around if I gave him a few min-utes to bitch about it first. I was right.

"This is what you want?" he asked in that tone of his that suggests supreme resignation on an epic scale.

"Yes!" I replied. "It will make taking care of the ducks so much easier!"

He bought the caddy. But putting it together was another matter entirely.

The assembly instructions – for a simple hose caddy – were written in Sanskrit, a language neither of us was familiar with. Putting the thing together by process of elimination – "This leftover piece *has* to go there because we've run out of other places to put it!" – we managed by some miracle to assemble a bona fide working hose caddy. I trundled the thing out back, hooked the hose up to the spig-ot, and gave it a trial run. It worked perfectly.

Duddy hadn't understood what all the fuss was about be-cause he wasn't the one doing the daily duck chores. Without ever discussing the matter – because I already knew that the task would fall to me – I had taken on the daily responsibility of making sure the ducks had everything they needed. But with cold weather nipping at our heels, it became clear to me pretty quickly how much extra effort the daily chores would require in the dead of winter: the water bucket had already frozen solid several times, and given the fact that each of the three ducks seemed to poop fairly reliably every eighteen minutes, there was a lot to do – all of it in bitter cold with exposed soaking wet hands. The hose caddy would make the tasks much easier.

I quickly established my routine: wheel the caddy outside (it overnighted in the laundry room next to the litter boxes), hook it up to the spigot, drag a 50-foot length of hose over to the duck area, dump out the block of ice from the water bucket, refill the bucket, create a mud puddle next to the bucket so that the ducks could dabble, toss worms to Ethel and Boyfriend, and set out a bowl of tomatoes for Penny. Next, I'd hose down all the poops – and there were many! – then top off the bowls of duck feed and add some fresh water to the pond. Once I'd finished with all of that, I'd lug the hose caddy back inside the house. The whole routine took about twenty-five minutes.

The highlight of the mornings was the ducks, of course. Penny was always very happy to see me coming, knowing, as she did, that a tasty bowl of 'maters was in the offing. I'd call to her from across the yard, *"Penny-Penny Pekin!"* She would natter back at me with a variety of clucks, honks, and quacks, running back and forth in her excitement. Clearly, my morning visit was the best part of her day.

Ethel and Boyfriend were never *quite* as excited as Penny, but they'd usually pick up the pace as they made their way over from their straw bed by the fence, knowing that they were going to get their daily dose of worms. While greedy

Penny was occupied with her bowl, I would toss Ethel and Boyfriend two big fat worms each. After all three had had their breakfast, they would make their way over to the mud puddle for some dabbling. The puddle never lasted very long before being absorbed into the ground, so they made the most of the opportunity when they had it. I have no idea whether any of them actually found anything worth eating, but they clearly derived a large measure of satisfaction from the process itself.

After dabbling, at least one of them would take a dip on the pond. Penny was the most amusing to watch: she would dive deep – as deep as she could in a three-feet-deep pond – popping up a few feet away from where she had gone under. She would flap her wings happily as she dipped this way and that, and it was obvious that she well and truly enjoyed the feel of the water on her body. Ethel and Boyfriend were usually fairly utilitarian about their bathing habits; Penny was the one who took genuine pleasure in her baths, making her a joy to watch. As winter set in, though, those baths would become fewer and farther between, and who could blame them – in frigid arctic cold, even a duck could lose its enthusiasm for pond time.

BARN TIME

"Hey! Let's do lunch," I texted Mandy in December. "I haven't seen you since the wedding in June!"

"Yes, you have," came her indignant reply, "we went to dinner!"

"We did??? When?"

"August," came her answer.

"Not ringing any bells," I wrote, "did we have a good time?" I grinned as I typed, knowing that she would invariably roll her eyes at my obvious decrepitude.

"As a matter of fact, we did."

"Glad to hear it! Are you on break from school, yet?" Mandy was in the midst of studying for her master's degree in speech pathology at Whoville U. I figured I could snag her for lunch and some riding at the barn while she had free time on her hands.

"Yes. I can probably go next week. Let me know where and I'll meet you."

Dismayed, I texted, "Don't you want to experience the thrill of riding in my new used car?" I'd just traded my

'99 Honda four-door automatic for a Honda '01 five-speed manual coupe, and I was inordinately pleased about it. But Mandy had other things to do on the day we were meeting for lunch, and would, sadly, have to miss out on the excitement of riding in my new used car.

I grinned in satisfaction when I pulled into the Olive Garden parking lot and found that rare gem, a parking spot right in front of the door. Once inside, my phone alerted me to a new message. "Where are you?" Mandy wanted to know.

"Inside, waiting for you. Where are you?"

"Outside. Be right in." The hostess escorted us to a booth, where we settled in for our usual round of gossip.

"Have you ever had days where human beings just piss you off to no end?" I inquired.

"All the time," she replied, "why?"

"I came across a woman today whose murder would've been worth the prison time!" I replied, then proceeded to tell her what had happened.

I was walking across the parking lot toward the County mental health facility that supplies my medications. There was a woman some distance away, walking across the same parking lot. She had a small dog on a very long leash – so long, in fact, that the little bugger got uncomfortably close to me. Mind you, I *like* dogs. I particularly like *well-behaved* dogs owned by well-behaved owners who keep them on short leashes. Such was not the case with the woman in question.

I opened the door to the building without bothering to hold it for the dog woman – who was still some distance back in the parking lot; only her dog was near the door. The door closed before he could enter. Behind me, I heard the woman take exception to what she clearly thought was incredible rudeness on my part: "Yeah, o.k. *thanks a lot!* Nice, real nice! Yep, thank you so much!" And on in this vein even as she let herself and her dog into the building. Calmly, I turned toward her and said, "You're welcome," which seemed to shut her up for a time. Bullies rarely continue when challenged.

I was then, as I always am in these instances, completely mystified by her verbal attack. She had no idea whatsoever that I was the local Critter Lady. For all she knew, I could have a dog-related phobia; I could easily have been frightened by the close proximity to her dog. And yet she seemed to think that I was obligated to like the little fellow as much as she did. I may well be a Critter Lady, but I don't owe everyone with a dog on a leash undue consideration. Indeed, the less-well-mannered the dog, the less I want anything to do with it. Or its owner.

The incident had rankled even after I'd come to the realization that I wasn't the only one availing myself of the County mental health services: clearly, the dog lady had issues, too, and was there for a reason! Mandy grinned in understanding as I pointed that out. "I should've strangled her with the damned leash!" I concluded.

Changing tack, I asked, "So when can you come out to the barn and ride with me and Bit? It's been *forever* since you've been there!"

"I *know*," she sighed, "School's been keeping me *really* busy! And all this arctic cold stuff isn't helping!"

"I *know!*" I commented, unconsciously echoing Mandy, "It was so cold, I missed two Saturdays! I can't function when it's fifteen below zero! But," I added hopefully, "it's supposed to warm up in a week or two. Maybe you'll still be on break then."

"I *definitely* want to ride before I go back to school!" she said emphatically.

"Let's plan on it, then. Just let me know which day." Mandy promised to get back to me.

I suppose there's something telling about the fact that I get along better with a 20-year old than I do with most 40-year olds. While I hope it doesn't mean that I'm embarrassingly immature, I confess that it's taken me an awfully long time to grow up; my emotional maturity was stunted at a very young age. Happily, neither my young, or my older, friends hold it against me.

PEKINS: NOT JUST
FOR DINNER ANYMORE!

It was almost 9:00 p.m. on New Year's Eve when my cell phone rang. When I answered, I heard a lot of background noise and then Lynnette's voice. She and Dave were presently in a restaurant somewhere in Florida, and it turned out she was in an agony of indecision because the menu featured an entrée of Peking duck. Lynnette liked duck. She liked making jokes about eating ducks whenever we dined out in Whoville. She was calling me now to inform me that because she had a friend who owned a pet Pekin, she felt constrained to order something else, something non-fowl. Cow, perhaps. *"Damn you!"* she said, laughing.

"Penny thanks you!" I replied smugly.

"If you ever adopt a cow, we stop being friends," she informed me.

"Fair enough!" I said. I wished her a Happy New Year and hung up the phone. Then promptly texted her a picture of Penny along with the caption, "Pekins: not just for dinner anymore!"

THE BIG CHILL

A few weeks into the New Year, a weather event of such monstrous magnitude happened that numerous records were broken, and numerous people died. Cold air came down not from Canada but from the Arctic Circle itself, blanketing almost half the country with record amounts of snow, as well as record amounts of cold: on the most dreadful day of all, the "high" in Whoville only reached -7 degrees. The lows, helped along by wind gusts of over 35 mph, hovered in the -30's. Newscasters took pains to remind their viewers that in such frigid conditions, frostbite could set in after only four minutes of exposure. Suffice to say, it was not fit weather for man or beast.

My first worry was for the three ducks in our yard. I had initially situated Dud's duck pen in the northwest corner of the back yard. Neighbor Russell's garage provided a useful windbreak, along with a red maple tree and a couple of old growth lilac shrubs. It was the least-exposed area we had to offer. I spread a couple of flakes of straw in the corner near the fence because I'd see the ducks huddled there a few times. It wouldn't be sufficient for the coming cold, but I was at a loss for what else to do. As an afterthought, I tossed a few handfuls of straw inside the pen, too. That afterthought turned out to be just the invitation the ducks needed: when the mercury began to drop precipitously, the ducks – all three, all voluntarily – wandered into the pen and took up residence. I was amazed.

To make sure it wasn't just a brief fit of madness on their part, I walked out back as night fell, pretending that I had some pressing business in the shed. Mostly, I wanted to get a peek inside the pen without actually approaching and disturbing them. To my considerable surprise, they were not only comfortably ensconced, huddled at the back, but they were in more or less the same position the next day, as well. Indeed, for the four-day duration of the worst of the weather, they only ever came out of the pen briefly, to eat and drink the fresh water I poured to replace the frozen chunk from the day before. After a meal, a good long drink, and a modest bit of preening, they would all waddle back into the pen and hunker down again.

I literally could not have been more pleased had you paid me money! That Ethel and Boyfriend, in particular, understood the need for shelter, and made the life-saving choice to avail themselves of the pen that had been the site of so much fear upon their initial arrival cheered me no end. I came away impressed with their level of intelligence, and I think Dud did, too. He certainly felt a long-overdue reward for his pen-building efforts. But while our ducks were well-taken-care of, there were others who did not have the benefit of shelter, and them I worried about helplessly as I watched the temperature drop and McKinnon's Pond ice over.

I emailed Jon Watson, asking if there was anything we could do for the ducks. The fountain had long-since been vandalized, and last-year's aerator was broken. Jon emailed back, telling me as compassionately as he could that he had his hands full with the storm – Whoville remained at a Level Three Snow Emergency for three agonizingly long days, in which anyone caught driving on city streets could be fined $500 – and wishing me luck in whatever I ended up doing for them. When the driving ban was finally lifted, I took a large plastic storage container down to the pond, and Dud and I went door to door with a bucket until we found a nice woman at home who was willing to fill it for us, but none of the pond residents had any idea what a water bowl was for, which meant that none of them ended up using it.

Around this same time, Aimee Van Staten emerged again. I didn't realize that she knew Liz, my weekend duck feeding volunteer, but the animal rescue circle is apparently a small one, and Aimee joined Liz for a feed in the midst of the winter storm. A round of emails began, then, as Aimee set a rescue plan in motion for the pond ducks. She'd had two successful duck rescues in recent weeks, and clearly, on the heels of those, felt that the time was right for someone to finally get the McKinnon's Pond ducks off the water for good. She'd even enlisted the help of Animal Control Officer Dave.

When Dave talked to me, though, he sounded unenthusiastic about the timing of the rescue – the wind chill on the day we spoke was -25 – and in the course of our conversation, he decided to postpone the attempt for a day or two. When I relayed that news to Aimee, her response surprised me.

"Well, I'm pretty pissed!" she announced, seeing her rescue attempt thwarted in one fell swoop. I think she thought that I had talked Dave out of doing the rescue, but nothing could've been further from the truth. Since she had the time off work due to the Level Three road status, and since she'd lined up several warm bodies to help her, I encouraged her to go ahead with her attempt. "I simply can't afford the physical cost (brutal, record-breaking cold)," I told her, "let alone the financial cost (a $500 ticket). But you go ahead!" I wasn't sure where we'd left things – her anger had shocked me – so I gave it a couple of hours and then called Dave for an update on their rescue attempt.

"We never even tried," he told me. Given that there was at least a foot of snow on the beach, and that the wind, having no windbreaks in the area, would have been blowing off the pond with a wind chill of minus thirty-something, I wasn't particularly surprised.

While they'd been out in the elements debating the wisdom of risking frostbite in the course of an animal rescue, Duddy and I had spent the time mildly puzzled by Aimee's sudden interest in rescuing ducks that had been living on the pond for well over a decade. "Where was she when you were paying their medical bills all that time?" Dud asked.

"Beats me," I shrugged.

"It's like she just wants to take over," he said.

"You know what, though? *Let her!* I've been taking care of those ducks for thirteen years! I'm more than happy to have someone else helping out! It doesn't bother me in the least." Which wasn't entirely true. When I turned the matter over in my head, I realized that what bothered me was the fact that Aimee hadn't even tried to avail herself of my experience with catching pond ducks. I knew my guys, after all; knew their habits, knew the terrain of the pond area, and the weather conditions; knew what was needed to improve our chances of success. But she'd never asked.

I tested the waters the very next day, emailing Aimee and telling her that I was going to go down to the pond as soon as the Level Three was lifted to bring the ducks a bucket of fresh water. Did she want to help me? As it turned out, the heat had gone off in her house and she was stuck waiting for the repairman to come. That didn't stop her from asking a series of questions about my water supply plan, though. "Are you getting a warmer, or does the City have some sort of hook-up?" she asked. "I don't think putting water out there without a warmer is going to help because it will freeze up so quickly." It was then that I realized what the problem was. The problem was Apollo 13.

As anyone who's seen the movie knows (and I'll ask your forgiveness if I get the details a bit wrong, here; I'm relying on Duddy's ability to recall the parts that I cannot.), the lunar module lost power. This was disastrous because not only would the astronauts lose heat – and potentially freeze to death – inside the module, but they would be unable to re-enter Earth's orbit, as well. In desperation, a group of brainiacs at Mission Control took a pile of odds and ends and jerry-rigged a potential fix for the astronauts. The pile contained only things that could be found in the module. It was a considerable challenge, which required those involved to think outside the box.

A similar dichotomy existed at McKinnon's Pond: Aimee was looking at the situation as someone who fully expected others to have whatever aid was needed, while I was looking at it from the prism of experience: there were no warmers, no City heaters – the ducks had never been the City's responsibility anyway – and no easy fixes; there was only me, and whatever I could think up to try to help. And at that point, the only help that came to mind was the storage container which, I suspected well before I'd put it in place, would remain unused owing to the ducks' distrust of anything new. All this, of course, was predicated on the assumption that the ducks had survived the onslaught of arctic air.

Knowing, as he no doubt did, that I had spent considerable time worrying, Officer Dave was kind enough to drive by McKinnon's Pond on day three, while the Level Three was still in force, and give me an update on my guys. "They're still alive," he assured me, which cheered me no end: they had survived the worst of the cold and wind chills, giving them a good chance of surviving until the pond thawed, which, if the forecasters were right, would happen in three more days' time. The task at hand, then, was to keep them going until the thaw, and this I worked on by dumping their cracked corn meals into the loose snow, guaranteeing that the ducks would ingest snow at the same time as corn, which would hopefully supply them with enough water to get them through until it rained, which was the next adventure that Mother Nature had planned.

We had not abandoned the rescue idea. Officer Dave called a day later to tell me that he'd spoken with Jon Watson, and elicited Jon's help in reviving the plastic fencing plan that Dave and I had used to rescue those six Pekins a while back. It would be the best way to corral them, we agreed, rather than trying Aimee's rather vague plan of chasing the ducks around the beach. Jon would arrange to have a couple of the Streets Department workers go out and set up the fencing, promising to try to get to it in a week or so – by which time, I hoped, the rains would have fallen, and the temperatures would have risen, making the attempt much less volatile than one done in minus twenty-five degree weather. In the meantime, I emailed Jon with some thoughts on placement and positioning of the fence.

"We'll need something half-moon shaped, with enough extra fencing that once the ducks are inside, we can close it up into a full circle. I'm assuming that the snow will be gone by next week, so maybe put the fencing six-odd feet away from the edge of the pond. Anywhere down in front of the boathouse would be fine. And then cross your fingers!" Jon's response was a cheery, "You bet Kelly. I will pass along your advice to our design team!" I think he was relieved to know that the ducks would be going to actual homes, which meant that he could finally ignore the issue of the broken fountain without any pangs of guilt.

With all of my thoughts centered on the weather, and the details of the rescue, I never stopped to consider what life would be like after the ducks were gone. I'd taken care of them for so long that not having that responsibility in my life anymore was unimaginable. And, to be honest, I didn't think Aimee was likely to catch them anyway, which meant that I wouldn't have to deal with the prospect of a change that was unwelcome to begin with.

CABIN FEVER

As days and weeks of record cold weather turned into months of virtual hibernation, I began to worry about Bit. Specifically, I worried that he would think I'd abandoned him. It had happened before, when his previous owners left him at The Harmony Barn when they decided that they didn't want to pay for his EPM treatment. I'm not convinced that that owner treated Bit well, so being left at the barn may well have come as a relief to him. He and I were pals, though, and I didn't want him thinking that I was never coming back to the barn.

Owing to the brutal cold, I elected *not* to volunteer on two successive Saturdays in February. Even with all the doors closed against the wind, it was still dangerously frigid in the barn, and my extremities tend to go numb fairly quickly. The third Saturday of that month warmed up to an almost-toasty 35 degrees, though, and I loaded up my pockets with not just my usual molasses-flavored horse snacks, but two sweet, crunchy apples as well. They were Bit's fa-vorite. I spent a fair amount of time, after mucking out was done that day, plying Bit with snacks and explaining about how the cold weather had kept me away. He seemed to take my explanation in stride.

It was that same day that Wendy told me that Fancy, a retired barrel racer, had been adopted. The same people were thinking about adopting Angel, too, but that had yet to be determined, so I didn't think any more about it. Angel was Bit's girl, a high-maintenance little thing who couldn't bear to be left with the herd when I took her boyfriend out for a ride. Ron clued me in to the idea of putting Angel in a stall by herself where she could feel safe, and it worked a treat: she kept relatively calm, and Bit, in his turn, could relax and work with me, rather than worry about whether the herd was picking on her in his absence. As with most things that seem abstract, so, too, did the possibility of Angel being adopted – abstract, that is, right up until it actually happened.

Nothing seemed different from any other Saturday, with the notable exception that several times, as I went from stall to stall in my mucking chore, Bit came and stood by the gate, whinnying as he did so. It was then that Wendy mentioned that both Fancy and Angel had gone to their new home, and I realized that Bit wasn't just randomly whinnying; he was trying to locate his girlfriend. *Aw, jeez,* I thought, *how am I going to explain this to him?*

Angel was a rescue horse from a neglect situation. She had come in with four others from the same barn. Wendy had segregated them from the rest of the herd, housing them in the front barn where the volunteers could frequently be found grooming them and plying them with treats. None of the horses was particularly social, and had to learn in their own time that humans could be trusted. Four of them figured this out; Angel never seemed to. Every time the volunteers descended on the front barn, Angel would turn and walk away, keeping at least one or two horses between her and the humans. She never really seemed to warm to any of us.

The couple – a Mr. and Mrs. Wayands – who had been "caring" for the horses had been charged with animal cruelty, with species ranging from dogs, to goats, to fish in a fishbowl. Evidently, they didn't actually own all five of the horses that were in their care, and after the trial, in which a cocky, over-confident young prosecutor lost on *every single one* of the 43 counts of cruelty he had charged the couple with, most of the horses went back to their original owners. When Mr. Wayands went to The Harmony Barn to retrieve the one horse – Angel – that he *did* own, once he'd seen for himself that she was getting top-notch care at Wendy's barn, he decided to let her stay. Which, of course, begged the question, *how little had he care about her all along?*

One person who really took to Angel was volunteer Michaela. An experienced rider, Michaela was away at college during the week, but managed to get herself out to the barn most Saturdays. Once the mucking chores were done, she could be seen trudging, lead rope in hand, toward the mud lot in search of Angel. If she turned left out into the lot, and if you waited a few seconds, you were guaranteed to see Angel trotting in the opposite direction. If Michaela turned right out into the lot and you waited, eventually, you would see the same thing in reverse: Angel trotting swiftly in the other direction. She was not inclined to be caught.

It took some perseverance on Michaela's part to actually catch Angel. Wisely, she never actually *chased* the horse, but rather, walked slowly and deliberately in pursuit until she eventually managed to corner the skittish creature. Once under saddle, Angel was every bit as skittish and anti-social as she was in the mud lot. This never seemed to deter Michaela, though I never knew if it was because she liked a challenge, or because she felt she was actually building a relationship with the horse. Of all the horses in the barn, Angel was probably in the bottom three in terms of popularity among the volunteers. Several had ridden her; but only one – Michaela – had enjoyed it.

I turned the matter of Angel's adoption over in my mind. I knew that there was nothing I could say to Bit that would make sense. Bit's an intelligent fellow, but human language was completely inadequate to the task at hand, and I hadn't yet learned to speak horse. The best I could offer were the "I know, Bubby, I understand," murmurings that were meant to somehow console him. I seriously doubt that they did. Hoping to distract him, I told him that I'd be back in a couple of days when it warmed up enough to ride, but it never actually *did* warm up enough to ride, which rendered my promise meaningless. Things just weren't going our way this winter!

It wasn't just the cold and the snow. I would have happily walked him on a lead rope up and down the driveway, just to break the monotony, but there was far too much ice to safely do anything like that, and I was not inclined to risk him pulling a muscle or worse, skating around on the ice. There was very little that Bit and I could do until it warmed up – and by "warmed up," I mean until the temperature rose above 30. Mind you, thirty is still pretty damned cold, but it is at least do-able. Unfortunately, the Weather Gods – who were clearly a twisted, sadistic bunch of bastards – wouldn't see fit to raise the temperature in Whoville until well into March.

During such record-shattering cold weather, all my regular activities ground to a halt. This meant that I ended up spending more time than usual inside my head, which was never a good idea. Without distractions to occupy my mind, flashbacks happened more often, as well as that recurring nightmare in which someone keeps trying to kill me. In the midst of all that insanity, the shrink and I decided that adding an additional psych med was in order. It was time to finally get the whole bat-shit-crazy thing under control.

THE END OF AN ERA

Well before Jon Watson had assembled his team of fence builders, Aimee Van Staten swooped down and effected a mass duck rescue at the pond. She didn't even wait for the arctic blast to pass, but rather, descended with her team of volunteers – including one highly-regarded avian vet – in the midst of the frigid cold. Apparently taking her cue from the fencing idea I had put forth, the assembled rescuers corralled the entire group of domestics into an L-shaped privacy wall that extended out from the boathouse men's restroom door, and grabbed them up from there. They managed to catch all seven ducks on the first try.

Not knowing about the rescue, I was on my way to the pond to check on the ducks when Aimee texted me. Now that the Level Three had been lifted, she wanted to know whether I would go and do a head count and ensure that all the domestics had in fact been captured. I pulled into the boathouse parking lot and texted her to stand by. I walked down to the shoreline, calling my usual greeting, "Ducks-ducks! Where's all the ducks? Come on, ducks! I've got *corn!*" But no one came. Of the fifteen-odd ducks on the ice, not one was a domestic. Aimee had, indeed, caught them all. I texted my confirmation to her, took one last look around McKinnon's Pond, then got back in my car and headed home.

Later that same day, I called Officer Dave. I knew the ducks were being housed temporarily in his state-of-the-art critter holding facility, and I knew that Aimee was planning on getting the ducks to their new home as soon as possible.

"Can I stop by and say good-bye to my guys?" I asked Dave.

"Absolutely!" he replied, "bring your camera and I'll get some pictures." Dave knew me well.

I hadn't been to the new holding facility yet and was keen to get a look around. In addition to the expected dog runs, there were also cages for other species – cats, raccoons, etc – separated from the runs by a solid cinder block wall, so that while all the animals in the cages could *hear* the animals in the runs, they wouldn't actually be able to *see* one another. In addition, there were rolled-up hoses hanging conveniently from the walls, and grated troughs in the floor where all the waste would run handily into. In a separate area stood a much nicer washer and dryer set than I myself owned. "Confiscated from a drug dealer," Dave said when I looked at him questioningly.

"Sorry?" I didn't quite understand what he meant.

"Seized in a raid on a drug dealer's home," he explained, "if they can't produce receipts showing they paid by credit card..." he trailed off.

"...then they probably paid for it with drug money," I finished for him.

"Exactly," he replied, "at which point we can confiscate it, which we did, and here they are!"

"Nice!" I responded.

"It's a cool way to get good stuff," he grinned in agreement.

We talked more as I hunkered down next to the dog run containing my gang. They were terrified – fear of strange things trumped even familiarity with me – and cowered together at the back of the run. I knew better than to get any closer or try to calm them, because it only would have scared them more. So I crouched nearby, talking softly while Dave took pictures. This was, I realized, the last time I would ever see Big Boy, Freckle, Peeps, Nipper and the rest. I had cared for them for so long that I couldn't take in the idea that I'd never see them again. It would, I knew, register later. For now, it simply seemed like any other time I had visited a duck at the vet's – they on one side of the cage, and I on the other, trying to reassure my charges.

Before I left, Dave tried to tempt me into adopting a kitten. There were two in the kennels, both black, but both possessing entirely different personalities. Dave pulled the extrovert from its cage and held it out for me to take. "Wouldn't you just *love* a cute little guy like this one?" he asked enticingly.

"This is the problem with having a spouse," I said by way of reply, "I have to run things by him now!" Dave laughed along with me, knowing exactly what I meant.

"Yep," he commented, "the spouse has to be considered!" I figured that was the voice of experience talking, given that his wife must surely have had an opinion on all those orphaned ducklings that got raised in their swimming pool.

"Dud doesn't like all the animals?" he asked.

"I think it's a matter of feeling outnumbered," I chuckled, repeating Duddy's anguished comment about not getting any say in the critter decisions. "I told him he could say all he wanted to," – by now, Dave and I were both laughing again – "but that he didn't get veto power!" We grinned conspiratorially as I put the kitten back in the cage. He was indeed a cute little guy, but my four at home were more than enough, and I couldn't see adopting another any time soon. We wandered outside, then, saying our good-byes as we parted company. "It's the end of an era," I remarked as I walked to my car.

Dave nodded his head in agreement, "yep," he said.

"Until someone dumps the next one." I let that statement hang in the air, knowing as well as Dave did that our optimism over the rescue of all the domestics would no doubt turn out to be short-lived.

Over the next week or so, I wrestled with a number of negative feelings that I didn't like having. Dud wasn't much help in this regard because he seemed to feel much the same as I did, and he verbalized those feelings a number of times. "She just barged right in and took over," he exclaimed yet again.

"Yes, she did," I replied vaguely. There was no point in denying it, for Aimee Van Staten had, indeed, done just that.

"She didn't even *ask* you, she just pounced on *your ducks!*"

"Yes," I said again, "she did just that." But how could I possibly complain when the woman had rescued them? How could I feel anything but foolish over the fact that while I had taken care of them all those years, I'd never made any real attempt to find them a home? Apart from the five lame drakes who had ended up at the Mitchell's, I'd left the rest of them on the pond. I couldn't even begin to count how many I'd lost to predators over the years because of that fact. Why hadn't I done what she did? I was the Duck Lady, for heaven's sake! This turn of events was as much embarrassing as it was anything else. And, they weren't really "my" ducks, either, even if I did think of them that way. Anyone was free to do what Aimee had done. It was just that, in thirteen years, no one ever had.

The home Aimee had found for them, the place that agreed to take in all seven of them, turned out to be a farm animal sanctuary in eastern Ohio, which meant that I could no doubt go visit them any time I chose, assuming I could talk Duddy into making the drive. I could already hear his voice in my head: "You want to drive *two hours* to visit ducks?!" The idea that our good-bye at Officer Dave's facility might not have been the final one cheered me somewhat. Even so, I continued to wonder why I hadn't thought of the idea of a farm sanctuary myself. It took me a while to come up with an answer.

Because I enjoyed them just where they were, that's why. Aimee saw them as creatures who needed rescuing, while I saw them as creatures who needed my care. Aimee's purpose in life was critter *rescuing,* while my purpose was critter *caring.* Two different sides of the same coin, when you think about it.

Having chewed on the matter at considerable length, I sat down with Duddy for a chat. "I appreciate your support," I prefaced, "because I was feeling the same way you were: put-out and annoyed. Aimee came into my territory unasked and whisked my ducks off to a new home. But I can't be angry about that because she did the right thing. I'm mostly angry at me for not doing it myself; I can't fault her for doing the right thing."

"I agree," Dud replied, "I just know how much you care about those ducks."

"Yeah, but it's good that they'll have a safe home for the rest of their lives, and I can finally relax and stop putting 'FEED DUCKS' on my daily list of things to do. I've got the three here, and that's enough."

"If Aimee had let you choose," he countered, "which ducks would you have brought home?"

Without hesitation, I easily answered, "the two that are already here, Ethel and Boyfriend. They became my favorites after Pretty Boy died. So with them, and now Penny as well, I'm good. I'm happy. We have the three best ducks out of all of them. I *might've* considered bringing Big Boy, too, but it would've been a huge problem during mating season, and we would've had to provide separate quarters away from Boyfriend, and it would *not* have been worth the hassle."

"So we're good?" Dud asked.

I nodded. "Yes," I replied, "we're good!" And I meant it. The only thing left was to wait for the pictures that Aimee promised the sanctuary would send. In the meantime, I tried settling into the idea that, for the first time in over a decade, my services would not be needed at McKinnon's pond.

It would take time to get used to, although Mother Nature unwittingly had a hand in the process: one after the other, she flung multiple arctic blasts down from the north. Ohio would suffer a surfeit of snow and frigid temperatures for weeks on end, only to have a brief respite – and at this point, fifteen degrees Fahrenheit was actually considered a respite – before the next blast swept through. Schools closed not only because of the copious amounts of snow, but also because, on a number of occasions, it was dangerously cold outside and no one wanted to be responsible for thousands of children getting frostbite on their way to school. Under such extreme conditions, it was just as well that the McKinnon's Pond ducks had finally been rescued.

✝

A Shot at Redemption

For those in the 12-step community, Step Nine is one of the most important. In fact, making amends to the people you've harmed is *so* important, you're meant to work your way slowly but surely through the first eight steps before you even *think* about Step Nine. And while it may seem obvious to the rest of society, saying "sorry" isn't usually very high on an addict's list of things to do, which is why the founders of AA decided to make it one of the necessary steps toward recovery.

In my own life, though I burned innumerable bridges with friends and acquaintances, the idea of apologizing never even occurred to me. I simply shrugged my shoulders and moved on, leaving countless people in my wake. Such is the nature of dysfunction: one turns into a tornado that flattens everything in its path and keeps on going. As time went on, though, and decades passed, and I got more therapy under my belt, I came to see that I owed at least *one* person an explanation, even if she wasn't interested in hearing it. That person was my old high school friend, Leslie.

While I had a modest circle of friends, back in the day, Leslie was my all-time favorite, and the one I spent most of my time with. We were on the Whoville High gymnastics team together. We experimented with underage drinking together. We got into all kinds of mischief together. Hell, we even showered together – back in the days before people thought things like that were strange. We were small town girls, imbued with the same small town sense of intimacy and familiarity as our parents, our neighbors, and the rest of our mates.

Unbeknownst to my mother, I tried teaching Leslie to drive her VW Bug. Leslie couldn't quite master the art of the stick shift, but she gamely gave it a try on a number of occasions around the acre that was our back yard. If we happened to see neighbors looking in our direction, we would duck down under the dash so that it looked as though the Bug was driving itself in those crazy circles. Indeed, Mrs. Grosskopf from three houses down called my mother once to tell her that *someone* had taken the Bug for a spin in the yard, but she couldn't say exactly *who!*

One of our favorite things to do involved putting on some of my mother's slutty 70's-era clothes, and then putting on her bras over the top of them, and maybe a pair of her undies, as well. If we were in particularly high spirits, we'd fill some zip-lock bags with water and stuff them in those bras, and then we'd parade around the driveway out by the road. Mind you, we were doing this in our *teens!* There was a pervy neighbor up the street who would always slow down and wave at us leeringly in our hooker-like garb. As his car passed, Leslie – always the braver of the two of us – would whip out her zip-locks and fling them at his car.

Another favorite activity involved raking up all the leaves that the maple tree out front had shed. We'd pile them up under one of the tree branches. The branch hung a good ten feet above the ground. We'd climb the tree, shimmy out onto the branch and wait. As a car drove by, we'd hurl ourselves off the branch and down into the leaf pile. The driver would slam on the breaks, thinking that some child had accidentally plunged to their death, when in fact we'd done the thing on purpose and had pretty much perfected the art of the safe landing.

And then there was Dougie Harman, the neighborhood weirdo. Dougie was several years older than we were, but still living at home in the way that young adults who are emotionally troubled tend to do. I don't think that his only – or worst – problem was being gay; I think his worst problem was that he simply wasn't likeable by virtue of the fact that he spoke in a shrill, imperious manner and tended to be a little bossy. I believe it was in the midst of the Blizzard of '78 that Leslie and I, bored and looking for fun in all the wrong places as usual, came up with our snowball idea, and the idea involved Dougie.

Before Dougie's parents bought him the Dodge Dart that he became so fond of, he used to drive their giant, gas-guzzling 70's pimpmobile. The car was ridiculously huge, having been designed back when oil was an infinite resource and the gasoline made from it was plentiful and cheap. The car was so huge, in fact, that it took no time at all for Leslie to catch on to my idea that we should start rolling a snowball around the yard. When it got big enough, I told her, we could roll it right up to the road – right up to where Dougie's pimpmobile would back into it, coming out of the driveway across the street. Even now, I can still hear us laughing in my head!

I should probably tell you that while my own upbringing left a lot to be desired in terms of rules, boundaries, and structure, Leslie's did *not!* Leslie came from a close-knit Catholic home in which the parents are still, to this day, happily married to each other. Leslie and her four siblings were taught good manners, and right from wrong, at a young age. Happily for me, though, she was usually willing to set all that aside for a bit of mischief.

In any case, Dougie must have been watching us from the bay window of his parents' house because just as we were putting the finishing touches on the giant snowball, he came mincing down the driveway toward us, swearing and accusing us of doing exactly what we'd been doing – trying to block his egress with our snowball. I recall trying to run away from the ensuing confrontation – I was a big wimp underneath all my bluster and bravado – but there were three feet of snow on the ground and it soon became clear that I was going nowhere fast. Leslie, though, in her usual role as tough guy, refused to break up the snowball as per his orders, and instead simply told Dougie to get lost. After Dougie ratted us out to my mother, she looked at us and burst out laughing. No one else among my friends made my mother laugh as much as Leslie and I did.

At some point in Leslie's young life, her maternal grandmother moved permanently into their house on Pine Street. Given that the three-bedroom ranch already held two adults and five kids, it became necessary to add a second story. This was divvied up into two large bedrooms – one for Leslie and her older sister, and one for Grandma. Separating the two bedrooms was a full bathroom. Just off Leslie's room was an unfinished area under the roof which housed a furnace. Given that my mother's house was heated by radiators, that upstairs furnace was a bit of a novelty for me.

I remember sleeping over at Leslie's, lying next to her in the big bed and feeling soothed by the white-noise roar of that furnace. I can still recall how, late one night, in the dark, choking back tears, I told her that her family felt more like my family than my own blood kin did. She could not have known, then – because the memories of my father's abuse hadn't surfaced yet - how important that feeling of kinship with her family was to me.

It wasn't all fun and friendship, though. After a period of smooth sailing, something would set me off, a slight, perhaps, or a perceived wounding where none actually was, and I would stop talking to her for a few months. After a period of time had passed, we'd simply rejoin forces without ever discussing what the problem had been. I couldn't have told her if I'd wanted to: my rage was unfocused, inexplicable. It would be decades before I figured out, with the help of a therapist, what all the anger was about; at the time, I knew only that my anger was like gasoline – highly flammable – and my friends were like lit matches.

We lost track of each other for a few years after high school before getting back in touch. After college, Leslie settled in Cincinnati for a time, and after my first marriage failed, I moved there, myself. We saw each other regularly, as time and differing schedules allowed. We were young women, then, getting our first taste of adult living, adult choices, and adult responsibilities. Leslie fared much better in this regard than I did: she had a career job, while I waited tables. She had a career income, while I made do with tips. She had a normal boyfriend and a normal life – just the sort of thing you'd expect from someone who grew up in a normal home.

I, on the other hand, floundered. Unsuitable boyfriends came and went, just like the dime-a-dozen restaurant jobs I plowed through, never working for one place very long. Once I butted heads with management, I usually quit without warning, robbing myself of a reference for the next job but not caring because it all seemed so pointless. What did it matter which restaurant employed me? The sore feet, rude customers and poor pay were the same no matter where I worked. At night, alone in my apartment, I took to drinking cheap red wine and crying myself to sleep. It was a half-life, an existence, but little more. There was no joy, and there was certainly no bright future to look forward to.

In the end, Leslie married that normal boyfriend – they're still married to this day – and I married husband #2, moving away from Cincinnati then and dropping Leslie altogether in yet another fit of anger for reasons I can't even begin to remember now. Suffice to say that the older I got, the bigger the chip on my shoulder became, and the more I withdrew from old familiar things. I didn't talk to Leslie again for 25 years.

After two-plus decades had passed, and I'd done a considerable amount of work with my shrink, it hit me one night as I sat alone in my chicken coop home: I had behaved badly. Many times. And I was sorry. And I should tell *her* that I'm sorry. This was huge. It had never occurred to me before that I might need to atone for my behavior. I sat there with a hundred different thoughts swirling in my head like flurries in a snow storm, understanding little about this new revelation but that it was terribly important and needed to be done. Soon. Now.

So I wrote her a letter. Long and rambling, I tried to explain myself, and my regret. I don't know how well I succeeded, but I kept writing until I thought I'd written enough. Then, because I had no idea where she lived, I sent the letter off to her mother, asking her to please forward it. Not long after, I got a letter from Leslie in response, saying, *in toto*, that she hadn't always been easy to get along with either. It was a charitable response, and more than I could've hoped for. Subsequently, I took to sending her a birthday card every year, and she took to sending a Christmas card which also mentioned my birthday, which she usually forgot. After all those years of silence, though, it hardly mattered that she forgot. What mattered was that I'd finally done the right thing by her.

That's how it stayed for another ten years, right up until a classmate of ours was horribly burned in an accident. Leslie and I were Facebook friends by then, and had sent each other a number of messages regarding our burned classmate. Leslie was planning to drive into Whoville for a weekend to visit our comrade, and she was willing to make time to visit with me, as well. I looked forward to the visit with keen anticipation.

If you didn't grow up in a small town, it's a hard thing to understand. It's a little like Mayberry (if you're old enough to get the reference) and a little like the t.v. show *Cheers,* where everybody knows your name. There's a level of familiarity that goes with knowing everyone's business: the fact that Donnie Wilmer had gotten to third base with Debbie Severs, back in junior high, or that Winnie Wilkens got busted shoplifting booze in high school, or that Stan Donnelly only had one testicle. It wasn't that we particularly *liked* knowing everyone's business; we just *did.* And I find that, no matter how much time you spend living somewhere else – like a big city far away from that small town – the small town still lives on inside you, just like the John Mellencamp song.

Which meant that it really didn't matter much that Leslie and I hadn't seen each other in 25 years, because all of our Whoville experiences still lived inside of us: antagonizing neighbor Dougie; riding our bikes all over Whoville, and riding double on her bike after mine got stolen; walking to school together many mornings – and seeing the pervy old man who would wait for us, standing naked at his window until Leslie threw a handful of gravel at him and we ratted him out to the police; getting into trouble at my house, or behaving at hers – all the hours and days and years of time spent together transcended the time that we spent apart. We arranged to meet at a local coffee shop, and I wondered briefly whether I would have trouble recognizing her. I immediately dismissed the thought as ridiculous.

I walked into the restaurant and there she was, directly in front of me. She was thinner than I remembered her, and looking very pretty in her fiftieth year, flashing her familiar toothy smile as she recognized me, and in an instant, we were in each other's arms. We'd never actually hugged one another in years past, but in the midst of our embrace, I shut my eyes tightly and the word *"home!"* flashed through my mind. Indeed: seeing Leslie again was like going home, back to a happy place that never actually existed for me except when I was with my friends. For the duration of that hug, it was like the world had finally righted itself in some small but meaningful way, and for that, I was truly grateful.

We spent a couple of hours catching up on the details of our lives. She brought me up to speed on her parents and siblings, and I did the same. We talked about our burned friend and how we might be of use to her in her convalescence. And then we went off in different directions with a view to meeting again for dinner in a few hours' time. Our visit had been an easy one, but *I* felt a tad uneasy because I knew that something still needed to be said before she went back home to Illinois.

I took the opportunity that night, as Duddy paid the bill, and mutual friends Dale and Kathy – with whom Leslie was staying – lagged behind us. "Walk with me," I said, hooking my arm in hers and leading her away from the others.

"I need to say this thing," I told her, "I was a shit. For many years, I was a shit. Because of what happened in the past, I was angry a lot. Actually, it doesn't matter why, it just matters that I was a shit, and I'm sorry. It wasn't you, it was me. And I'm sorry."

She looked at me with wide eyes, then. She seemed hesitant, as though she didn't know how she should respond to this unexpected confession. Eventually, she said she didn't think that friends had to be sorry with friends – or words to that effect. In truth, I hardly heard them: my ears were ringing with embarrassment at the fact that it had taken so long for me to address my bad behavior. While my mind breathed a sigh of relief at having finally done the right thing, my heart was saddened by how many years of friendship I had missed with her. At the same time, I felt a small surge of optimism that we might move forward from there.

It may seem unimportant in the grand scheme of things, reconnecting with someone I hadn't seen since my early twenties, but here's the thing: she knows me. She's always known me. Even now, after all the therapy I've done, and all the changes I've made, she still knows the basic Kelly who lives underneath it all. The Kelly who gleefully thought up ways to torture the douchy neighbor, the Kelly who always knew how to make her laugh, the Kelly she shared many of her life's firsts with. And even though she's spent years out in the big world, living in a number of cities and states along the way, there is still a small-town girl within her, too, that I am intimately familiar with. It is, I think, the thing that binds us together and makes forgiveness easy. Well, *easier*.

I have no idea what happened to Dougie Harman. My mother has long-since traded in her suggestive 70's wardrobe for something more staid and comfortable. The Bug is long gone. Leslie finally got the hang of driving a stick shift when she bought her first car. I seriously doubt that I could do a handstand now, although she probably could since she hits the gym regularly. Her parents no longer live on Pine Street, and neither does my mother. Whoville doesn't much look like it used to anymore: Piatt's Bakery is gone, Mills Hardware closed recently after sixty-plus years in business, and there's now a ridiculously over-priced outdoor shopping mall over on the west side of town, loaded with expensive boutiques that no one really needs. Whoville's gotten a little too highfalutin' these days, and the small-town nuances are lost on the newcomers. Sadly, John Mellencamp's small town America is not so much, anymore. Which makes it extra-nice when you find that some of those old ties still bind.

LAURA, REVISITED

During a rare lull in that hideously cold winter, I ran an errand to the frame shop. I had a series of photos of Duddy falling backward off the dock of his friend Tommy's cottage in Omena, Michigan that I wanted framed. It would serve as an optimistic reminder that, sooner or later, even the worst winter would finally end. As I stood waiting for Laura to finish up with a customer, I glanced around the shop and took note of what had changed since the last time I was there.

It was hard to believe that two years had passed since Maxi the wonder dog died. It was even harder to believe that over a year had passed since new dog Tori had come on the scene. Tori, a black lab mix, had been recommended to Laura by the same woman who had fostered Maxi. To this day, Laura has no idea *why* the woman thought Tori would be a good fit: unlike mellow Maxi, Tori was a handful; enthusiastic and energetic, her high spirits tried Laura's patience on an hourly basis. The last time I'd been in the shop, the exhaustion had shown clearly in Laura's eyes.

She hadn't actually finished grieving for Maxi when she agreed to take Tori. Going on the assertion that Tori was several years old, Laura had assumed that Tori would be reasonably calm and well-behaved. In fact, she was entirely the opposite, and Laura had come very close to returning her on numerous occasions.

You could see the sorrow plain on her face. Laura usually played her cards close to the vest but losing Maxi had hit her hard, and she was by no means over the shock when Tori came into her life. And Tori was everything that Maxi was not: loud, ill-mannered, with a remarkable sense of selective hearing that allowed her to filter out unpleasant words like "no." Laura frequently found herself at the end of her rope, and it was clear that sometimes, she wished Tori would just disappear. Obviously, what was missing was a bond like the one she'd had with Maxi. But bonds take time to develop and the last thing Laura felt like doing in the midst of grief was working on building a new relationship.

It hardly mattered. Tori was so enthusiastic that she worked on building a relationship anyway, disregarding that impatience as just an odd, lovable quirk on Laura's part. In a unique turn of events, Tori took on Laura's role, slowly but surely encouraging her new human friend to come out of her shell and try loving again, just as Laura had done with Maxi when she'd first adopted her. As I looked both of them over on this visit, it was clear that they had finally reached some accord.

Time itself had helped the process. Laura had had Tori for over a year at this point, which gave them both plenty of time to figure out where they stood with each other, and what was expected of them. Laura hadn't taught Tori to do that victory lap around her work station yet, but she *had* come to the understanding that Tori wanted and needed to play; new toys were scattered all over the frame shop floor. And Tori had clearly learned that "no!" did, in fact, often mean "no." Both dog and human seemed to be breathing much easier than they had in those tense early days.

When her customer finally left, I sat on the work station table and chatted with Laura for some time. We both grinned, remembering how ill-mannered Tori had been when she'd first come to live with Laura. "There's no way that dog was anything *close* to three years old when I brought her home!" she exclaimed, "She was closer to one."

"She sure acted like an overgrown puppy," I agreed. "And you finally got her to stop jumping on people!"

"Well...not *all* the time! Not yet, anyway." And as Laura said it, as if reading our minds, Tori promptly jumped up and tried to give me a hug. I gave her a swift knee in the chest, just as Laura encouraged anyone to do when Tori tried jumping on them. The big dog got the hint, dropped to the floor and went off in search of a chew toy. She found a squeaky one, and chewed – and squeaked – happily as Laura and I looked on.

"She's not Maxi," I remarked, "but she's not so bad, now, either."

Laura nodded. "She's getting there. Slowly but surely."

And while she was still too excitable for me to give her treats, the UPS guy always came prepared, as did the Fed Ex lady. They, too, missed the calm and polite Maxi but they, too – just as I, and Laura's other regular customers did – embraced the new dog anyway. Because Laura's Frame Shop just wouldn't be the same without a dog.

Without realizing quite what was happening, my life started coming together like a giant jigsaw puzzle: I kept fitting pieces together, over the years, but I was never really able to see what the big picture was going to look like. The shrink knew, of course, but I, myself, couldn't see how a little Step Nine work here, and a little quiet contemplation there, were adding up to a certain completeness.

There would always be issues: ghosts of the past, problems of the present, and instances where change would happen slowly – if at all. But there was, indeed, a new and improved Kelly surfacing, someone troubled by the past but no longer strangled by it. The future was still unknowable, but the present had finally become livable.

Coming Full Circle

While I don't remember exactly what year it was, I can vividly recall a wintry Saturday in the midst of my adolescence. It was cold and snowy outside, and I was alone inside; my mother and brother were elsewhere. Because my mother was frustratingly cheap about the heating bill, our house was always cold, and the oven – long considered by her to be an alternate heating source – was almost always on. Such was the case this winter day.

I remember sitting on the edge of the kitchen sink, resting my feet on the open door of the oven just in front of me. My mother spent whole winters curled up on the floor in front of that oven door, reading books. I myself, with nothing to do and nowhere to go, was just killing time.

I had prepared a cup of tea. I don't recall when I became a tea drinker but I enjoyed a cup on this particular day. I was thinking about James Herriot, and the wonderful books about his veterinary practice in rural England. The Whoville Public Library had a large biographical tome about Herriot, complete with numerous photos of the Yorkshire Dales he so loved, called *James Herriot's Yorkshire*. I remember pouring over the pictures, intrigued by the beauty of the hills and the remoteness of the villages, and I fantasized about living in just such a far-away place.

That particular day by the oven, I was embroidering on those fantasies, imagining myself as Kelly, the World Famous Writer, living in a cozy cottage miles away from everyone – which meant, mainly, those in my family who had harmed me – along with my typewriter, camera, dog and horse. Up to that point in my life, I'd never been anywhere *near* a horse, and the only dogs I knew personally were the parade of toy poodles that my grandparents owned over the years. But the fantasy really appealed to that agonized child within me, and while I had absolutely no idea whatsoever how to make it a reality, that fantasy never left me; the desire to live far, far away from the rest of humanity remained somewhere deep within.

Recently, in the winter of my fifty-first year, I had some time on my hands one day while Duddy was out and about, and I found myself sitting in my upholstered rocking chair, a biography of James Herriot on my lap, staring thoughtfully into the snow storm outside and thinking back on that day by the oven in my mother's house. I was cozy warm there in my chair, having made it a policy, decades ago, that I would never be cheap with the heat in my own home. I watched the fat snowflakes falling, and took note of the fact that Penny, Ethel and Boyfriend were huddled out on the patio, slowly being covered with snow while they waited for a treat from me. And I realized that that long-ago fantasy had, with the odd exception, more or less come true.

I'd traveled to England seven times in my adult years. A couple of times, I took another person along with me, but mostly, I traveled alone. I adored those trips alone, savoring the exciting differences in that European city, soaking up the local culture, trying to blend in and be as one of them, riding around all day on the Tube, eschewing American restaurants like McDonald's in favor of the fare in local pubs. I happily walked the back streets and off the beaten paths, frequently getting lost but finding my way around a bigger whole in the process, unwittingly linking up one area of town with another as I roamed, and spending money left and right, buying up all manner of trinkets and souvenirs in the hopes that they would carry me through the dull regularity of my life back in the states.

Those trips to London were my salvation. In London, I was happy. In London, I was at peace – a rare gem I'd never seen the like of at home in Whoville. In London, I was who I was meant to be. But only for six nights. I would have loved to have stayed there, to have taken up residence, but I'd done my homework, and I knew that I would not be welcome unless I was independently wealthy – a thing, alas, that I was not, and did not imagine ever becoming.

So instead of a remote farmhouse in the Yorkshire Dales – or anywhere else in England, for that matter – I found myself in my cozy Critter Shack, having traded the fantasy of high-maintenance dogs for the ease of independent cats, three happy ducks outside, and my best pal Bit the horse only a five-minute drive away. And while the Critter Shack may not be located anywhere remotely remote, the *feeling* of space is there, thanks to that privacy fence that borders the property. It is the adult version of the child's dream.

Interestingly, in the fantasy, I always lived alone. It was a given that I would be alone. After all the years of having been violated by my father, *alone* is what I craved then, and alone is what I still prefer now. Imagine trying to comfortably fit a husband into that legacy! Some days I really struggle with having another human being in the house, and there are probably far too many times when I think in terms of "mine" instead of "ours."

I try to keep it to myself, but every once in a while, something slips out accidentally, like the time I mentioned, "You keep leaving your car keys on *my* side of the dining room table!" Dud hasn't yet mastered the art of raising just one eyebrow, but he sure was trying when I said that! And, in spite of my tenuous relationships with my fellow humans (the sixteen years with my shrink is the only long-term relationship that I've managed in my life) I confess that I *do* quite enjoy having someone – having *Duddy* – in my home – in *our* home, and in my life. He has been a godsend and a gem, two things I never expected to have.

At the same time, I worry. I live in near-constant fear that the thing I cherish and value most in the world – Duddy – will be lost to me. Every night, I pray that we be allowed to have a "long healthy, happy marriage," and every day, I worry that I will somehow lose him. I worry most about a car accident. Having endured being molested for most of my formative years, I learned early on that nothing good ever lasts, and that bad things will always outweigh good ones. While I have finally come to believe that I deserve a wonderful man like Dud, I have a lot of trouble *trusting* my good fortune. Trust was always a dicey prospect back then, and it still is to this day.

Happily, though, the basic elements of my original adolescent fantasy have come to pass: I have the house, the typewriter (computer), the camera, the horse, and the other assorted critters. And I have one thing that I couldn't imagine factoring into that dream all those decades ago: I have my *sanity*. As well, I have the promise of a good life with a man who is well and truly my best friend. If things don't always sail smoothly between us, we are at the helm *together*, and we're enjoying the trip immensely.

If there is one thing I would have you take away from my story – apart from the universal message that *all* species of animals are deserving of our kindness, compassion, and consideration – it is this: that while the *conservative* estimate is that one in four girls will be sexually abused before their 18th birthday, and one in six boys, the current belief is that it's one in *three* girls, and one in *five* boys. Those numbers are horrendous. If those were the statistics for any type of cancer, we would've somehow found a cure by now, or at least a fairly decent treatment. In addition, according to my therapist, who gets her information from FBI data, the average pedophile molests over 120 children before he's caught. Let that number sink in a bit before you keep reading. 120 children violated *before* he's caught. That's a lot of kids.

And in spite of the ubiquitous "CHILDREN SHOULD BE SEEN AND HEARD AND BELIEVED" bumper stickers, the fact is that children are *not* being believed nearly often enough – and certainly not when the accused is a well-known figure. Michael Jackson a child molester? *Never!* But then, why was he isolating children on his property away from their parents, and feeding them a wine/soda concoction that he nicknamed "Jesus juice" to make the beverage sound more credible?

Jerry Sandusky, assistant football coach at the legendary Penn State University, guilty? *Certainly not!* But how convenient that he started a children's charity and stocked it with impoverished boys who would happily lap up all the lavish bribery he bestowed upon them. Because *that's what child molesters do!* That's what priests and musicians and fathers and football coaches do: they bribe and cajole, and more often than not they ply their young victims with drink and drugs in order to make them more malleable.

The longer we deny the epidemic, the more furiously it rages, fueled by the anonymity of the internet, by society's willingness to turn a blind eye, and in equal measure, by its refusal to admit the truth. Cardinals and bishops *knew* what their priests were up to, but instead of protecting the children, they consistently chose to protect the pedophiles, by quietly moving them to other parishes, rather than reporting them to the police. In the case of Jerry Sandusky, those who suspected told the wrong people, and those wrong people *chose to do nothing.*

Worse still, there are untold millions of non-offending parents who either suspect something is happening, or know for a fact that it is, and choose to turn away from that knowledge. Where you would think that they would immediately jump to their child's defense, more often than not, they don't. In trying to maintain their own physical or emotional survival, the non-offending parent ends up sacrificing the child in the process. And there is nothing worse than a child being betrayed by both parents.

What can you do? Take it seriously. *Believe.* Given the statistics, you, the reader, either *are* a childhood sexual abuse survivor, or you *know* someone who is. If you are one, get help immediately, and stick with it until you feel your life is under control. If you know one, believe them. I've heard an astonishing number of stories, over the years, from people I would never have suspected of being survivors, and not one of them has ever given me a reason to think that they're lying.

I can tell you from my own personal experience that there is *not one thing* in it for me if I lie. What I mean to say is that I would gain nothing if I made up a lie about being molested. There would be no monetary gain, or any other kind. Equally, I gain nothing by telling the truth: the truth alienated some, and I assume that I have been written out of more than one will because of it. I only ever told the truth because my sense of integrity wouldn't allow me to continue pretending that others' lies were the truth when they were not. Even if certain family members never believe me, *I know the truth*. And I will continue to speak the truth in order to help myself and others.

Childhood sexual abuse truly is an epidemic. Did you know that pedophiles frequently travel to places like Thailand because they know that they can easily procure young children for sex with impunity there? If that doesn't disgust you, it *should*. Pedophiles make and trade videos over the internet of themselves and others violating children. And let's not forget the Elizabeth Smarts of the world, children who were kidnapped for no other reason that to satisfy a pedophile's sick urges. Child molestation is out of control and must be faced, and dealt with. Mainly, I think that means stricter sentences for pedophiles, and some sort of accounting/punishment for those who shield them. Because, as I've said previously in this book, *there is no cure for being molested!*

Having said all that, I'd like to end on a happy note, although, when I thought about *how* to end on a happy note, the only thing that came to mind was to simply list the wonderful characters who have colored my world, put a smile on my face, and brought me immeasurable joy. So here goes:

Pretty Boy Duck! And his fondness for George Harrison songs.

Miss Muffin, and her clandestine ability to catch the odd mouse.

The gang at McKinnon's Pond, who spent years cheering whenever they saw me coming.

My buddy Ruckus, who taught me so much about horsemanship.

My new best pal Bit, who continues my equine education.

Cranky donkey Cricket, who was loved by everyone, in spite of her many moods.

Buddy, Spanky, Junebug, and Gracie, who continue to share my life, my home, and my heart, and who were willing to let Dud into their lives, as well.

Jon Watson, for his willingness to be part of the solution.

Animal Control Officer Dave, for his unfailing kindness, and cheerful nature. Please don't ever retire!

New friend Lynnette, who appreciates duck lovers as much as she appreciates duck dinners.

Old friend Leslie, who is one of the few welcome links to the child I used to be, and is now a happy link to the future.

My nameless therapist, who figured that we'd spent enough time in her office, over the years, that she was willing to break with the protocol that dictates keeping a professional distance and attended my wedding. Not to mention putting up with me for 16+ years!

And, of course, the one person who makes all things seem possible, my wonderful husband Duddy. I had no idea that life could be this good until you came along, Dud! I owe you so much, but mostly, I owe you my gratitude for taking on not only me, but my cats, the ducks, and that barn-full of ornery horses! *Thank you!*

Last, but certainly not least, thank you, dear readers, for coming along for the ride. I hope you feel that the time you've spent here was worth the price of my book, and I look forward to sharing still more animal stories with you in Book 3. Until then, please be kind to critters!

EPILOGUE

The bird fluttered into my periphery as I sat reading on the couch. Absently, I glanced up just in time to see a red-tail hawk fly onto a low branch of the red maple tree in the back yard. That maple tree was in duck territory, and although all three ducks were currently lounging on the patio, the hawk was still much too close for comfort. Instantly, I flung myself up off the couch and raced to the sliding glass door.

"Don't even think about it!" I yelled as I raced across the patio, waving my arms over my head as I ran. The hawk took one look at the crazy woman sprinting toward him and flew off, winging his way over neighbor Russell's house.

"What was that?" Duddy asked vaguely, still half-absorbed in his own book.

"A hawk," I answered. "A *huge* hawk. I scared him off, though." Dud went back to his reading, and so did I. A few minutes later, though, another flutter caught my eye, this time, coming from beyond the privacy fence at the back of the property. "Good Lord!" I squawked, "that's an eagle!

Look at the size of him!" Dud glanced out to where I was pointing.

"No way!" he said.

"Just look at that wingspan! It's gotta be six feet across!" Dud shrugged. "Maybe," he considered. Six feet or no, I wasn't taking any chances. I went back outside. Running toward the fence, I waved my arms above my head again and hollered, "Bugger off, you bastard!" Prey animals have skewed vision in which objects appear larger than they really are. I was hoping that the same thing was true for predators, too, because the eagle was so high up in that tree behind our property that I really didn't pose much of a threat to him. Thankfully, he decided to move along anyway, no doubt flying off to places not inhabited by crazy critter ladies. Dud and I settled back into our reading again, though my mind was no longer on Stephen King's Overlook Hotel.

Duddy hadn't reacted much to my attempts to scare off the hawk or the eagle. He didn't even bat an eye when I ran full speed across the patio, waving my arms like a mad woman. Chuckling to myself, I realized that by now, he surely must have become accustomed to the level of passion with which I attended to my critter responsibilities: cleaning out the duck pen was never a tedious job, but rather, one filled with wonder at how smart the ducks had been to know that the pen would shelter them from the worst of the winter weather, and a near-constant level of amusement at just how much poop three ducks could manufacture in the course of one day. Feeding times were always joyful occasions, in which Penny, in particular, would natter and quack her end of the conversation while I happily chattered mine in response.

For the most part, the ducks spent the daytime hours huddled on the patio, that first winter, close to the food and water bowls that I had to keep chipping the ice off of.

Duddy and I spent most of those days busy in the house, unaware of the everyday minutia of outdoor critter life. But they were always on the back burner of my mind, and come what may – whether it be dealing with an arctic blast of frigid weather, or dashing through multiple feet of snow – I was prepared to do *whatever* it took to protect my innocent charges. Even if it *did* mean running around the yard waving my arms and hollering like a lunatic. Which is probably why Dud didn't seem terribly surprised: because he knows, by now, exactly who and what he married. The Critter Lady may have finally found a measure of sanity in her life, but clearly, there remains enough *in*sanity inside to still qualify as Crazy! Happily, Duddy doesn't seem to mind a bit.

First Place Blue Ribbon Champion Horse

(Bonus Chapter)

"I think I pulled an ass muscle when I was mounting Bit today," went the text I sent to Mandy, "I tried mounting from the right and almost fell off the other side! Apparently, my leg overshot the saddle."

"Nice!" came the reply, "I bet that was something to see!"

"I managed to catch the saddle horn at the last minute," I told her.

"Why would you mount from the right?" she wanted to know.

"Because Stacy Westfall says to train from both sides, so I tried. It's gonna take some practice!"

"But you don't need to train both sides for your purpose," she said.

"Bit doesn't know that!" was my inarguable reply.

Given that I'd already set the precedent by getting Bit that First Place blue ribbon, it was only a matter of time before I loaded him up with a few more. Over a period of weeks, his stall door came to be decorated with a First Place ribbon, a Best of Show rosette, and a Grand Champion ribbon as well. In addition, I tracked down a woman on Etsy who was selling off the ribbons her mother had won long ago, and managed to acquire for Bit a couple of First Places from 1959! Considering the fact that Bit hadn't actually earned any of the ribbons in proper competition, the barn volunteers found it all highly amusing.

"Hey!," I'd tell them, interrupting their mirth, "Bit earned those by being the Best Horse Ever! And that's *quite* an accomplishment!"

"But the ribbons have some other place listed on them," Wendy remarked, "they're not from *our* barn."

"These two here," I replied earnestly, pointing at the older ribbons, "date from the late '50's. That's before your time, Wendy, so naturally, they wouldn't be Harmony Barn ribbons." I was having trouble keeping my grin in check, and so was Wendy as she responded knowingly, "I *see!*" The barn kids just tittered; they were used to my weirdness.

"You guys should see the trophy I have at home! It's *huge!*" I had also found the trophy on Etsy, a solid metal horse – unlike the cheap plastic ones they make now – atop a large Bakelite base, circa the National Golden Horse Show, Springfield, Missouri, 1948. I had seen something similar in a book on English home decor: a large, beautiful equine trophy gracing a study in some old English country home. It was just the sort of thing that would look perfect in the front room of the Critter Shack – the room that Dud and I were slowly renovating in the style of a country cottage.

I realize that the usual way to do these things is to take your horse to a competition, actually *compete,* and hope that you're a better rider than the other contenders. But life hadn't worked out that way for Bit or me: Bit's contesting days were cut short by his EPM diagnosis, and I was nowhere near skilled enough to enter competition. Still, I saw no reason to let those facts stand in the way of accomplishment. For two years, I had worked with Bit – mostly patiently, and sometimes not – on the ground and in the saddle. We had put in a lot of hours together, and it struck me that that fact alone should be rewarded. Bit had worked hard, and had never once behaved maliciously. Yes, there were times when he screwed up royally – the run through the neighbor's cornfield after seeing the plastic bag being blown around on the breeze springs notably to mind – but for the most part, he seemed to pick up on what I was trying to teach him. Slowly but surely, Bit's learning a few things about being bombproof.

It helps immensely that there is actually a book on the subject, called, handily enough, *Bombproof Your Horse,* by Sgt. Rick Pelicano. I bought my copy on the used book website AbeBooks.com. I was beyond pleased when I leafed through it and found that, quite inadvertently, I had come up with several bomb-proofing exercises that Pelicano used in his book. Happily, we were on the right track, and I continued Bit's education as Spring finally thrust its head up from the frozen earth. Given that Bit continued to assert his status as Alpha Horse (which meant my putting up with a *lot* of resistance – not to mention attitude – on his part), it was often hard to see the results of our labor. I knew that he *was* making progress, but I didn't always know *how.* Until, that is, the day that Wendy announced that he'd won a Grand Champion trophy.

I had turned up half an hour late for Saturday barn duty. There was an errand that needed running beforehand, which put me off schedule. When I finally wandered in, Wendy said she had something for me. I walked over to where she'd left the thing, on top of the tool box. The only thing I saw on top of the tool box was a horse trophy, dated 2008, announcing on the name plate, "OIHA Grand Champion, Division 3."

"*Division three, no less!*" I enthused, when in truth, I had absolutely no idea what (or where) Division 3 was, never mind what 'OIHA' might stand for.

"*Ohio Interscholastic Horseman Association,*" Wendy informed me, "We never used the trophy back when I was coaching the equestrian team."

"I'm not meant to take this home, right?" I asked with some confusion.

"No, you can have it!" Wendy replied, "Bit definitely earned it!"

As it happened, Bit and I had been doing some bomb-proof training just the day before, which involved me riding him up to the end of the driveway and having him stand still while cars drove by. We hadn't actually made it to the *end* yet – we stopped about fifteen feet away from where the driveway met the road – but it was still close enough for a horse who'd spent his life being afraid of his own shadow. I would have him stand still for a minute or two, praise him for his patience ("*Way to stand still, Bubby! Good job!*"), then turn him around and walk him toward the back barn.

The notable thing about that day's driveway walk was that it was witnessed by riding instructor Connie, who was, apparently, impressed enough to mention the incident to Wendy. But Wendy had her own story to tell: during that same training session, as Bit and I walked back down the driveway, the UPS man came driving up. This was just the sort of scary thing that I wanted Bit to become accustomed to, so I turned him around until he was facing the road again, and brought him to a halt.

He was back far enough that the UPS truck wouldn't come too close, but he was close enough to it that he would wonder whether or not to be scared. He decided not to be scared, which was what caught Wendy's eye: that flighty horse of hers who used to spook constantly at things real and imagined, was standing stock still while the UPS guy backed his truck down the driveway. Evidently, Connie and Wendy had traded stories and had both come to the same conclusion, that Kelly was actually getting somewhere with Bit. The Grand Champion trophy made it official.

While I was thrilled (we had actually earned something that I didn't have to buy!) *and* amused (Wendy was getting into the spirit of things!), I had actually had my own "ah-ha" moment a few days earlier that no one but Duddy knew about.

We had been riding up the driveway toward the street. We were just passing the front barn when I heard a familiar noise, that of plastic rustling in the breeze. I saw the cause of it mere seconds before Bit did: the noise came from strips of plastic that were stuck to a forklift and flapping in the wind. In the nanosecond before Bit turned his head, I thought, "Oh, crap! That's going to be a problem!" Except that it wasn't. Bit merely looked, assessed, and kept on walking. No spooking, no attempts to run away, no nothing. Just a solid horse making a sensible judgment based on experience. Based on what he'd *learned* from his experience. In addition to being really gratifying, it was a huge step forward! My flighty friend had finally learned that the whole world was *not*, in fact, out to eat him. You could've knocked me over with a feather!

As is almost always the case – at least for me – I was so intent on the various trees that I was unable to see the forest itself. Bit *had* been learning from me all this time, I was just too close to the subject to be able to see it clearly. Every once in a while, though, the Gods throw me a bone to let me know that I am, indeed, getting somewhere. And the fact that a day later, we won a trophy for our progress just put the validation icing on the cake. Bit and I were finally becoming a *team*.

Is he "cured" now? Totally bombproof? No. And I don't think he ever will be. The training will continue, though, every chance I get, in ways that you wouldn't even think constituted training: lately, I've enlisted barn volunteer Lydia's help by having her walk along with us with a balloon tied to the back of her pants, and carrying a riding crop with a plastic grocery bag attached to it.

I've instructed her to randomly wave the crop around as we walk, so that there's always an element of surprise for Bit to contend with. In addition, I regularly confront Bit with various uncertainties and obstacles, such as the rolled-up wad of carpeting lying in Wendy's side yard. While Bit continues to shy away from the terrifying patch of dirt in an otherwise grassy lawn, he seems to have no compunction about stepping over that rolled-up carpeting.

Bit and I will continue to train because we both like a challenge. When I started working with him two years ago, I had no idea that we would actually make any progress because I was making it all up as I went along. Who knew that someone with as few horsemanship skills as I possessed could actually train a horse of Bit's caliber? Now, though, having seen what he's capable of, I will encourage him to be what I already know that he can be: a first place *blue ribbon* champion horse!

Kelly Meister-Yetter is a writer, photographer, blogger, and author of *Crazy Critter Lady*. She shares her life with three ducks, four cats and a barn full of ornery horses. Based on her years of experience rescuing animals in need, Kelly also acts as an advocate for their care and humane treatment, donating her time and resources to numerous animal welfare organizations. When she's not volunteering at a horse rescue facility, Kelly enjoys training her horse, and waiting on her cats hand and foot. Kelly, the critters, and her husband live in Northwest Ohio.

You can find Kelly at www.crazycritterlady.com.

Made in the USA
Columbia, SC
30 May 2017